GUIDE TO
Pennsylvania's
TOURIST RAILROADS

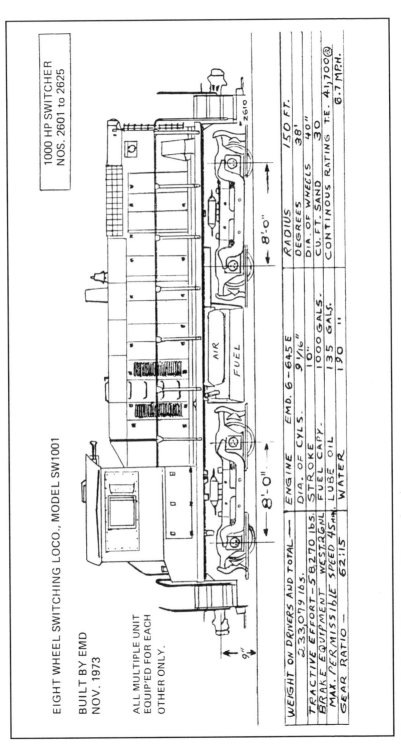

EIGHT WHEEL SWITCHING LOCO., MODEL SW1001

BUILT BY EMD
NOV. 1973

ALL MULTIPLE UNIT
EQUIP'ED FOR EACH
OTHER ONLY.

1000 HP SWITCHER
NOS. 2601 to 2625

WEIGHT ON DRIVERS AND TOTAL —	ENGINE	EMD. 6-645E	RADIUS	150 FT.
233,079 lbs.	DIA. OF CYLS.	9 1/16"	DEGREES	38'
TRACTIVE EFFORT—58,270 lbs.	STROKE	10"	DIA. OF WHEELS	40"
BRAKE EQUIPMENT WESTR.GNL	FUEL CAP'Y.	1000 GALS.	CU.FT. SAND	30
MAX. PERMISSIBLE SPEED 45MPH.	LUBE OIL	135 GALS.	CONTINOUS RATING T.E. 41,700@	
GEAR RATIO — 62:15	WATER	190 "		6.7 MPH.

8'-0"   8'-0"   9"

AIR   FUEL   2610

Courtesy Railroad Museum of Pennsylvania

GUIDE TO
Pennsylvania's
TOURIST RAILROADS

Bill Simpson

PELICAN PUBLISHING COMPANY

Gretna 1998

*The word "Pelican" and the depiction of a pelican are trademarks
of Pelican Publishing Company, Inc.,
and are registered in the U.S. Patent and Trademark Office.*

Library of Congress Cataloging-in-Publication Data

Simpson, Bill, 1950-
    Guide to Pennsylvania's tourist railroads / by Bill Simpson.
      p.   cm.
    Includes index.
    ISBN 1-56554-267-3 (pb : alk. paper)
    1. Railroad museums—Pennsylvania—Guidebooks. 2.
Pennsylvania—Guidebooks. I. Title.
    TF6.U5S55 1998
    385'.074'748—dc21   97-25095
                                                    CIP

*Information in this guidebook is based on authoritative data available at the
time of printing. Prices and hours of operation of businesses listed are subject
to change without notice. Readers are asked to take this into account when con-
sulting this guide.*

Manufactured in the United States of America

Published by Pelican Publishing Company, Inc.
1101 Monroe Street, Gretna, Louisiana 70053

*To Dad and Uncle George—
may you forever be together
on the trolley to Terre Hill*

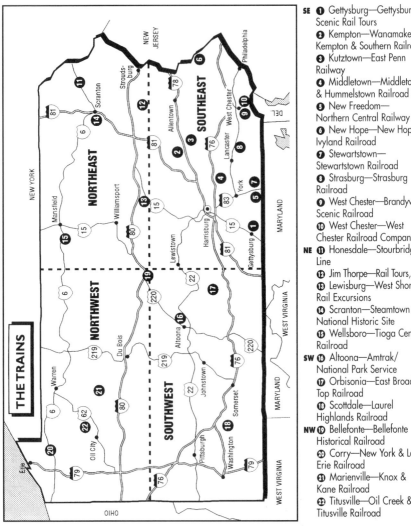

THE TRAINS

Map by Linda Eberly

Contents

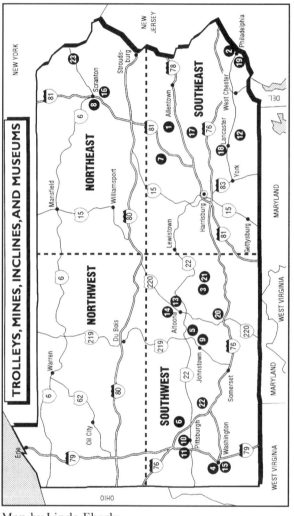

TROLLEYS, MINES, INCLINES, AND MUSEUMS

Map by Linda Eberly

TROLLEYS

SE ❶ Kempton—Berksy Trolley
❷ Philadelphia—Welcome Line Trolley
SW ❸ Rockhill Furnace—Shade Gap Electric Railway
❹ Washington—Pennsylvania Trolley Museum

COAL MINES

SW ❺ Patton—Seldom Seen Mine
❻ Tarentum—Tour-Ed Mine
❼ Ashland—Pioneer Tunnel Coal Mine
NE ❽ Scranton—Lackawanna Coal Mine

INCLINES

SW ❾ Johnstown—Johnstown Incline
❿ Pittsburgh—Duquesne Incline
⓫ Pittsburgh—Monangahela Incline

RAILROAD MUSEUMS

SE ⓬ Strasburg—Railroad Museum of Pennsylvania
SW ⓭ Altoona—Altoona Railroaders Memorial Museum
⓮ Cresson—Allegheny Portage Railroad National Historic Site
⓯ Washington—Pennsylvania Trolley Museum
NE ⓰ Scranton—Steamtown National Historic Site

SMALLER MUSEUMS

SE ⓱ Leesport—Reading Technical & Historical Society
⓲ Manheim—Manheim Historical Society
⓳ Philadelphia—Transit Museum Store
SW ⓴ Robertsdale—East Broad Top Area Coal Miner's Historical Society Miner's Museum and Entertainment Center
㉑ Rockhill Furnace—Rockhill Furnace Trolley Museum
㉒ Youngwood—Youngwood Railroad Museum
NE ㉓ Honesdale—Wayne County Historical Society

Preface

Some people don't understand my fascination with trains. They don't understand why I feel disappointed whenever I come to a grade crossing and don't have to stop for ten minutes to watch a long freight train pass. They don't understand why whenever I hear a train whistle my ears perk up like those of a dog hearing one of those whistles that humans can't hear. They don't understand why I'd pull my bicycle to the side of the road to watch a 200-car coal train roll along the tracks beside the Susquehanna River. I don't know how to explain it, either. Some people just don't understand the most basic human emotions. Perhaps the following few paragraphs will help the doubters gain an understanding of the magic of trains.

In the simplest sense, they're nothing but utilitarian vehicles. They transport people and freight. They make noise and they stop traffic. They're not nearly as fast as airplanes, and they don't stop at South of the Border, Wall Drug, Taco Bell, or any of the other scenic sites along America's highways. So, to a person unable to appreciate the truly beautiful parts of our world, trains might seem like lumbering legacies of America's past.

As all train lovers know, however, trains are much more than mere utilitarian vehicles. They're transportation, technology, history, adventure, intrigue, song, and romance all rolling down "magic carpets made of steel," as Arlo Guthrie put it. The train was the world's first form of mass transportation, and for many generations of Americans, the train was the only way to travel. Whether they were marching off to war or going down to the shore, Americans traveled by train.

In small towns across America, life revolved around the depot. The train brought food, mail, clothing, and visitors, and it carried local farmers' and miners' goods to markets. The lonesome whistle of the midnight train inspired song writers and brought young men visions of travel to distant places. Movie producers used trains liberally, and trains became legends in their own time: the Broadway Limited, the Wabash Cannonball, the Orange Blossom Special. From the 1840s through World War II, trains and trolleys were integral parts of the daily lives of millions of Americans.

Cars have changed that, but trains still have a visceral appeal for many of us. Whether it's a ride on the East Broad Top or an afternoon spent watching mile-long freight trains struggling up Horseshoe Curve, trains captivate me and many others. That's why we have tourist trains. As regularly scheduled passenger service has declined, tourist railroads have stepped up to fill the need to ride the rails that so many of us experience.

For those of us with that need, Pennsylvania is the best place to be. Pennsylvania is a leader in tourist railroads because Pennsylvania was a leader in railroads. The first trip by steam locomotive in the United States took place in Honesdale in 1829. The construction of Horseshoe Curve, which opened in 1854, was one of the first great railroad engineering feats, and the Curve is still in heavy daily use. The Pennsylvania Railroad was one of the most powerful corporations in the world, and the Reading earned a place on the Monopoly board. Pennsylvania has a powerful railroad legacy, and Pennsylvanians have strong ties to their trains. The state has thousands of miles of train tracks, and some of those tracks are now finding work as tourist railroads.

If a friend or loved one has a fascination with trains, and you find that fascination perplexing, go for a ride on a tourist train. Watch the eyes of a child grow wide as a huge, hulking steam locomotive comes to life. Enjoy a meal as you roll down the rails. Watch the scenery pass slowly by, and think back to a time when a train was the fastest way to travel.

Trains are a link to our past, and they're also an important part of our present. Freight lines are carrying more cargo now than ever before, and while passenger service is in decline in the United States, it's an important part of the transportation system of most European countries.

Yes, trains may be lumbering legacies of a time when life moved at a slightly slower pace, and that's about as good a thing as anyone can say about them. In a hectic world, few activities are more relaxing than a 10 MPH stroll down the tracks. The train won't make the modern world go away, but it will help you block it out for a while.

Introduction

If all 50 states entered into a contest to determine which state has been most influential in the growth of American railroads, Pennsylvania would stand a good chance of winning. From the beginning, Pennsylvania has been a railroad leader, and many railroad firsts occurred here. The first trip in the New World by steam locomotive took place in Honesdale in 1829. The longest covered bridge ever built, 5,690 feet in length, carried trains across the Susquehanna River between Columbia and Wrightsville. In the first half of the 20th century, the Pennsylvania Railroad was as big and powerful as any in the world. The Pennsy owned more than 3,000 locomotives, 6,000 passenger cars, and 200,000 freight cars, and it served more than 2,000 cities from the Atlantic Ocean to the Mississippi River.

Despite the Pennsylvania Railroad's size and influence, it was not the only railroad in the state. The Reading, Baltimore & Ohio, Northern Central, New York Central, and many short lines operated within Pennsylvania, as did numerous trolley systems. Throughout the state, rails found their ways into big cities and small towns. Every settlement of any significance had a rail depot, and in many towns the train station was the hub of commercial activity.

Getting the rails into all those Pennsylvania towns wasn't easy. Pennsylvania's highest elevation is only 3,213 feet (Mount

Davis in Somerset County), but the state's topography features steep mountains that run primarily from north to south. Because the main routes of commerce run east and west, the mountains made the building of railroads, especially east-west lines, a real challenge. Railroad engineers had to be creative to cross the rivers and climb the mountains, and perhaps the most famous railroad engineering feat in the country resulted from that creativity. At Horseshoe Curve, located just west of Altoona in the center of the state, the train doubles back on itself to gain altitude as it climbs a mountain. Opened in 1854, the Curve is still in heavy use and a favorite spot for train watchers. While historians generally consider the completion of the transcontinental railroad the defining moment in American railroad history, it was the completion of Horseshoe Curve that really made further westward expansion possible.

Although Conrail trains still climb Horseshoe Curve every day, the Pennsylvania Railroad is just a memory, as is passenger service in most of the state. Amtrak runs one line across the southern tier between Philadelphia and Pittsburgh, and one daily train stops in Erie, but most towns in Pennsylvania no longer have passenger-train service. However, thanks to tourist railroads, you can still see many parts of the state, including many historic sites, from the window of a slowly moving train.

If you chose to ride all of Pennsylvania's tourist railroads, you'd see an interesting cross section of attractions, including such historic sites as

• America's most famous battlefield—Gettysburg Railroad
• America's first Amish settlement
• America's most productive non-irrigated agricultural county—Strasburg Railroad
• The route of America's first steam locomotive—Stourbridge Line in Honesdale
• The world's steepest incline—Johnstown Inclined Plane
• The world's first oil well—Oil Creek & Titusville Railroad
• America's second-highest (and formerly the highest) railroad bridge—Knox & Kane Railroad

• The nation's first refuge for birds of prey (Hawk Mountain)—Wanamaker, Kempton & Southern Railroad

• Pennsylvania's Grand Canyon—Tioga Central Railroad

• America's most authentic* tourist railroad—East Broad Top Railroad

• America's most entertaining railroad—Northern Central Railroad

And even if you don't care what's outside the windows, you'll enjoy riding the rails. So head for Pennsylvania and a wonderful collection of tourist railroads. The exact number changes annually, and 1996 was a year of extremely good growth. Five new tourist lines began operation, and enthusiastic riders flocked to all of them. Pennsylvania was a leader in the development of American railroads, and it's a leader in the development of tourist railroads. In the Keystone State, an eclectic assortment of tourist lines keeps the state's railroad history alive.

* While other tourist lines have brought in period locomotives and passenger cars from various locations, the East Broad Top is still using the same equipment that it's had since the 1910s.

Defining Tourist Railroads

Traditional railroads carry people and freight from one place to another on a strict schedule. In fact, in 1883 the railroads of the U.S. and Canada adopted the concept of standard time, and soon railroad time became standard throughout both countries. Thus, in many ways it was possible to set your watch by the daily train.

Tourist railroads operate differently. They run strictly to give passengers the pleasure of riding a train. They go down the tracks and back so that passengers can ride the rails and perhaps enjoy a meal. In many instances the same tracks carry both tourists and freight, and the railroad's identity as a freight line or a tourist line may depend on the day of the week. The concept of tourist railroads is hardly a new one. From the beginning, railroads have carried passengers who were riding simply for the thrill of it. Perhaps the first true tourist railroad began operating in 1872, when the Gravity Railroad in Mauch Chunk (now Jim Thorpe) stopped hauling coal and began to carry only passengers. For more than 50 years the Gravity Railroad functioned as a tourist railroad.

In this book, you'll read about tourist lines, Amtrak, and other railroad attractions in Pennsylvania. Train service isn't what it once was, but in Pennsylvania you can still enjoy riding the rails.

The Trolleys

Trolleys, streetcars, interurbans. They've gone by many names, and they've been a huge part of rail passenger service in the United States. Once cities large and small had extensive trolley networks. Today the only streetcar systems still running in Pennsylvania are in Philadelphia and Pittsburgh. However, in several locations you can still enjoy rides on old-time trolleys and visit trolley museums. You'll find restored trolleys operating in

• Kempton—Berksy Trolley
• Philadelphia—Seasonal tourist rides around Center City and Chestnut Hill
• Rockhill Furnace—Rockhill Trolley Museum and rides
• Washington—Pennsylvania Trolley Museum and rides

The Coal Mines

Railroads have served many purposes in Pennsylvania. One of the most important was (and is) moving coal. At these four sites, you can board a small train and travel into a real coal mine:

- Ashland—Pioneer Tunnel Coal Mine
- Patton—Seldom Seen Mine
- Scranton—Lackawanna Coal Mine
- Tarentum—Tour-Ed Mine

The Inclines

Mountains surround many Pennsylvania communities, and some of those communities built inclined railroads to provide the quickest possible routes from the bottom to the top. In the state, three inclines are still operating:

- Johnstown—Johnstown Inclined Plane*
- Pittsburgh—Duquesne Incline
- Pittsburgh—Monangahela Incline

* At 71.9 degrees, the Johnstown Incline is the steepest in the world and also the only one equipped to carry automobiles.

Railroad Museums

Many museums recount the history of railroading in Pennsylvania. At these museums, you can see what a rugged life working on the railroad was, and you can learn about the technical and engineering feats that made railroading possible, as well as how railroads have influenced life in Pennsylvania and beyond.

Pennsylvania's railroad museums come in different sizes and with different themes. Some smaller ones focus on railroading in a particular area. Others, such as the Railroad Museum of Pennsylvania, take a broader view. At the Railroad Museum of Pennsylvania everything has a Pennsylvania connection; trains either ran in Pennsylvania or were manufactured in the state.

Many museums are close to one of the tourist railroads, allowing you to ride a train and to learn something about railroad history on the same day.

Location, Location, Location

If you drove around Pennsylvania on the state's major highways, you wouldn't happen on many of the tourist railroads described here. Most of the lines are in small towns, and they travel through areas that are primarily rural. Of all the rides, only Steamtown, the Johnstown Incline, the Philadelphia trolleys, and the Pittsburgh Inclines are in "big" cities.

The operators of the Strasburg Railroad often receive phone calls asking how others can build a business like the Strasburg. The operators' answer is that it's helpful to find a site with heavy tourist traffic, beautiful scenery, and plenty of other tourist attractions nearby. Those criteria apparently eliminate every other site in the country, because Strasburg carries at least twice as many passengers as any other tourist line in the country.

The Strasburg benefits greatly from its location on PA 741 in the heart of Lancaster County's Amish Country, a major tourist destination. Other railroads located in regions that attract large numbers of tourists are the Tioga Central, the New Hope & Ivyland, Rail Tours in Jim Thorpe, Steamtown, and the Gettysburg. Perhaps farthest from beaten paths are the Wanamaker, Kempton & Southern and the East Broad Top. Coincidentally, those two lines offer the best chance to get cinders from a steam locomotive in your hair.

Don't Be Late

Although many of Pennsylvania's tourist lines are far from population centers, rail fans find them all. Sellouts are always a possibility, so be sure to call ahead if you're traveling to a train. As evidence of the attraction of the trains, consider these 1996 sellouts:

 • Tioga Central's Saturday dinner trains were sold out four and five weeks in advance
 • Laurel Highlands sold out many rides in October

• Stourbridge Line sold out its Halloween ride

What makes these sellouts noteworthy is that none of these railroads is anywhere near a major population center. So, be sure to call ahead to avoid disappointment.

What Are You All Steamed Up About?

Choo . . . choo . . . choo . . . choo . . . choo . . . choo . . . choo . . . choo. The sound of a steam engine is distinctive and enchanting. Once, coal- and wood-fired steam engines produced all the power that moved the trains that carried the nation's passengers and cargo. The sounds, the sights, the cinders, and above all the smells were integral parts of a ride on a steam-powered train. The smell of burning coal is the smell of history. It's the smell that built America.

Then diesel power came along. Diesel engines are more efficient and cleaner than steam, but steam has an attraction that diesels can't match. If a diesel train captivates everyone who sees it, a steam train is positively mesmerizing. When a steam train passes, everyone stops to watch, to admire, and to fantasize a bit. If steam were cheaper, just about every railroad would use it for tourist operations, but one railroad man estimated that a run that required $40 worth of diesel fuel would require $400 worth of coal, so the reason for using diesel is obvious.

Despite that expense, steam engines power many tourist trains, and steam is a great attraction. Few experiences in train riding can match a ride in an open car behind a steam engine. The black smoke drifts back, and the cinders fly everywhere. It's not a place to wear a white dress, but it's a great place to enjoy trains as they once were. In Pennsylvania, you can enjoy steam rides on these lines:

• East Broad Top
• Strasburg
• Steamtown

- Gettysburg
- Wanamaker, Kempton, & Southern
- Rail Tours
- Knox & Kane*
- Laurel Highlands
- New Hope & Ivyland

*Unlike the other steam lines, which use old steam engines, the Knox & Kane uses a Chinese-built steam engine from the 1980s.

Some Rail Great Food

In the golden days of rail travel, many trains were rolling luxury restaurants. Every long distance train had a dining car and a high-quality menu. Dining on the train was a formal affair that called for suits and dresses. Today, many tourist railroads recreate that dining experience, and you can enjoy a complete meal on some rides on these trains:

- Northern Central Railroad
- West Shore Excursions
- Strasburg Railroad
- Tioga Central Railroad
- Oil Creek & Titusville Railroad
- Middletown & Hummelstown Railroad
- New Hope & Ivyland Railroad
- Stourbridge Line
- Bellefonte Historical Railroad*
- Stewartstown Railroad*
- Gettysburg Scenic Rail Tours*

*On these trains, you won't actually eat on the train. The Bellefonte Historical Railroad carries diners to a restaurant on the last Friday of each month. The Stewartstown Railroad has Country Breakfast trains on one Saturday morning from June through November. Breakfast is at a small town restaurant along the line. Gettysburg Scenic Rail Tours' dinner trips offer either a chicken dinner at a volunteer fire company or dinner in a restaurant along the line.

On most lines, the dinner trains are special evening runs, and passengers don't have the option of riding the train and not buying the meal. The major exception is the Strasburg Railroad, which has its own dining car where passengers may order either lunch or dinner. On the Northern Central, every run centers around dining, and many trains also feature entertainment.

A typical train meal includes salad, meat, vegetables, dessert, and beverages. The food is quite good, and costs generally range from $25 to $35. If you prefer a vegetarian meal or have special dietary needs, call ahead. The railroads will work hard to handle your requests.

Pennsylvania's dinner trains have become quite popular, and many sell out well in advance. Make your reservations early to avoid disappointment.

Some Great Places to Watch Trains and Take Pictures

This is by no means a complete list. With more than 5,000 miles of track, Pennsylvania offers plenty of photo opportunities. The following are just a few sites where you'll get frequent opportunities to snap away.

Thompsontown, PA Route 333. Here, a major Conrail line runs beside the Juniata River. Long freight trains roll by with regularity. On average, at least one train an hour passes this way.

Downtown Lebanon/Hershey. A major Conrail line passes through Lebanon and Hershey. Freight trains are frequent at all hours of the day and evening.

Horseshoe Curve, Altoona. This is a tourist attraction with real trains. As many as 50 freights and at least half a dozen passenger trains go across Horseshoe Curve daily.

Special Events

Pennsylvania's colorful fall foliage is an occasion for special rides on almost every tourist railroad. Other themes include Easter, Halloween, Christmas, a reenactment of the Civil War, Mother's Day, Father's Day, the Harvest Moon, the Great Train Robbery, and the Pennsylvania German Festival. For just about every holiday or special day, some railroads have extra trains on top of their regular schedule, or have special activities on or associated with the rides.

Rent a Car

If you have a group outing, many tourist lines will allow you to rent your own private railroad car. You can have a formal dinner, a birthday party, or even a Super Bowl party. Almost every line will be happy to accommodate your group.

Getting Some Exercise

If you enjoy combining your train ride with some active recreation, Pennsylvania offers plenty of opportunities. With their rural locations, many tourist railroad stations are excellent beginning places for bicycling, canoeing, hiking, and walking. Here are some of the active recreation possibilities associated with the different trains.

Oil Creek & Titusville—A bike trail runs along Oil Creek from Oil Creek State Park to the Drake Well Museum. Passengers can take bikes or canoes on the train and return under their own power. The bike trail is about 10 flat miles, and the canoe trip is also about 10 miles. In summer, the creek is generally shallow.

Northern Central—This train shares a rail corridor with a 12-mile hiking and biking trail (with more under development). Passengers can take bikes on the train and ride back to the station.

Brandywine Scenic—The train runs a special canoe train in conjunction with a canoe rental company located at the station. The canoe ride is about 9 miles.

Wanamaker, Kempton & Southern—A park with tennis courts is adjacent to the station.

Rail Tours (Jim Thorpe)—Mountain biking and white-water rafting are popular in this region. A bike rental company is across the street from the train station, and the surrounding woods are full of trails.

Johnstown Incline—A hiking trail, two winding, steep miles long, goes from the lower station to the upper station. In some spots, the trail is extremely steep, so it's actually easier to walk or run up than down.

Tioga Central—Pennsylvania's Grand Canyon (with a 25-mile rail trail) is nearby, and the state parks on both sides of the canyon are excellent for hiking. Pine Creek is a favorite among canoe enthusiasts.

Knox & Kane—The Allegheny National Forest covers most of the surrounding region, and offers hiking, mountain biking, canoeing, and camping.

Gettysburg—A bike rental company offers tours of the battlefield with the rental package.

In addition, Pennsylvania has 103 state parks. They offer many types of recreation, and some have lodging. For a brochure on the parks, call 1-800-63-PARKS.

Out in the Open

On a warm day, riding in the open air is a pleasant way to travel, and many railroads make that possible with a variety of open cars. The following lines have genuinely open cars, meaning no roof:

- East Broad Top
- Wanamaker, Kempton & Southern
- Oil Creek & Titusville

These next lines have cars that are "open air." They have roofs but they're open on the sides:

- Strasburg
- Gettysburg
- Rail Tours
- Knox & Kane
- Tioga Central

Most Unusual Car

This distinction goes to the Gettysburg Railroad. The car is a former automobile carrier that's now a double-decked passenger car capable of holding 240 passengers. The upper floor definitely provides the highest passenger perch in Pennsylvania railroads, and it's the most popular location on the train. However, it does sway significantly from side to side. Honorable mention goes to the Northern Central's dancing car, which is a completely open car with a sound system.

When You're Riding More Than One

With a little planning, it's often possible to ride more than one train in a day. These trips are close enough to each other to make it possible to do two in one day:

- Brandywine Scenic and Strasburg
- Strasburg and Middletown & Hummelstown
- East Penn and Wanamaker, Kempton & Southern
- Wanamaker, Kempton & Southern and Rail Tours
- Rail Tours and East Penn
- Steamtown and Stourbridge Line

- Erie Limited and Oil Creek & Titusville
- Northern Central and Stewartstown
- Pennsylvania Trolley Museum and Laurel Highlands Railroad
- Pioneer Tunnel Coal Mine and West Shore Rail Excursions
- Johnstown Inclined Plane and Amtrak on Horseshoe Curve
- Duquesne Incline, Monangahela Incline, and Pennsylvania Trolley Museum

If you want to do three in a day, your best possibilities would be East Penn, Wanamaker, Kempton & Southern, and Rail Tours.

This Ride Brought to You by . . . Volunteers

At many of Pennsylvania's tourist railroads, volunteers play an important part in keeping the trains running and the museums open. Some railroads are entirely volunteer organizations, and some have both paid employees and volunteers. The volunteers give freely of their time and they're very helpful, so be sure to thank them profusely. Your words of appreciation are their psychic income.

Railroad History Teachers

If you're interested in the history of a line, just ask one of the conductors on the train. Generally, they're very interested in their trains, and they know pretty much everything about them. Once they take all the tickets, they're happy to talk about trains for the rest of the ride.

Pennsylvania's Weather

Not only did the railroad builders have to struggle to cross steep mountains and wide rivers, but they also had to deal with winters that could be quite harsh. Because of those winters, few of Pennsylvania's tourist railroads operate all year. In fact, only the Strasburg and New Hope and Ivyland operate all year, and even they limit their operations to weekends during the cold months.

In general terms, the tourist railroad season lasts from late March until Christmas, and the busiest month is probably October when Fall Foliage rides highlight the schedules of most railroads. The best weather months are September and October. They're usually warm and comparatively dry. The nicest month lasts from mid-September until mid-October.

Pennsylvania's weather has a clearly defined four-season pattern, but all sections of the state do not have the same weather. The Southeast, for instance, is measurably warmer than other sections of the state. Philadelphia's average temperature is about seven degrees warmer than Scranton's average.

Spring comes sooner and winter comes later in the region from Harrisburg to Philadelphia than in the rest of the state. Pennsylvania doesn't have a hot spot, but it does have an icebox—the region around Kane in the Northwest quadrant. The towns of Kane, Bradford, and Smethport take a curious pride in their low temperatures, and one of them is usually the coldest place in the state.

Every part of the state can be hot in summer, although truly stifling days are relatively rare. Average precipitation across the state is about 40 inches annually. In summer, the majority of the rainfall comes from afternoon thunderstorms.

Schedules, Fares, and Fees

They change. Before you depart for any of Pennsylvania's railroad attractions, call ahead. If you can't call during business hours, an answering machine will tell you when the trains are running or the museum is open. All prices in the book are for round trips (except for those specially marked for cyclists or canoeists taking the train in one direction only).

Glossary of Railroad Terms

Every industry has its own language. These are some of the terms commonly used by railroad men and women.

ABANDON. To cease operating a stretch of track. Many of Pennsylvania's tourist railroads operate on tracks that other railroads abandoned.

ARTICULATED. A steam locomotive with two sets of driving wheels under a single boiler. Articulated locomotives have wheel arrangements such as 2-8-8-4 or 4-6-6-4. A 2-8-8-4 has two small wheels in front, two sets of eight wheels in the center, and two sets of two small wheels in the rear. Usually, there will be only three numbers, such as 2-8-2. Only very large locomotives have four numbers. When that happens, the locomotive has two sets of wheels in the center. The numbers always read from front to back. The accompanying diagram illustrates a 4-4-2 configuration.

BLOCK. A section of track used to control trains.

BOOMER. A railroad worker who changes jobs as he drifts across the country.

BRIDGE ROUTE. A railroad with more bridge traffic than traffic originating or terminating on that line.

BRIDGE TRAFFIC. Freight received from one railroad to be moved by a second railroad for delivery to a third. Also called "Overhead traffic."

CLASS 1 RAILROAD. A railroad with annual gross revenue greater than $255.9 million.

CLASS 2 RAILROAD. Revenue from $20.5 to $255.9 million.

CLASS 3 RAILROAD. Revenue under $20.5 million.

COG RAILROAD. A railroad that uses toothed wheels on the locomotive meshing with a rack between the rails. Cog railroads

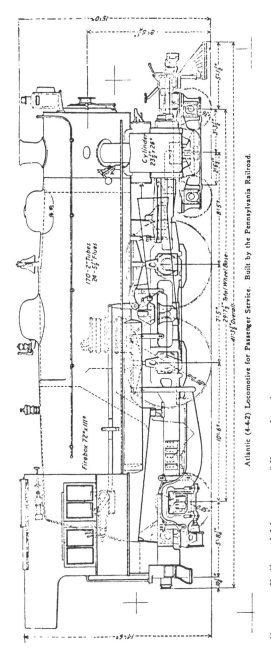

Atlantic (4-4-2) Locomotive for Passenger Service. Built by the Pennsylvania Railroad.

Courtesy Railroad Museum of Pennsylvania

allow trains to handle much steeper grades than traditional methods, but they tend to be very slow.

COMMON CARRIER. A transportation company that offers its services to all customers.

CONSIST (CON' SIST). A group of locomotives or the makeup of a train.

CONTRACT CARRIER. A railroad which carries goods for one shipper.

CROSSING. A special piece of track that allows two tracks to cross each other but does not allow trains to move from one track to the other.

CROSSOVER. Two track switches laid back to back to allow trains to move from one track to another parallel track.

CUT. A section of track that has been cut from the earth, often by blasting.

DEADHEAD. To travel in a train not to support its operation but to be in position for subsequent operations. Can apply to both equipment and workers.

DOUBLEHEADING. The use of two locomotives and two separate crews to pull a train.

DOUBLE-STACK. The transport of containers stacked two high on special cars.

FILL. A right-of-way formed by placing rock, earth, or other material across a low spot to form a flat area suitable for tracks.

FIRST-GENERATION DIESELS. The locomotives that replaced steam locomotives.

GEEP. Nickname for General Motors GP series diesel locomotives.

GRADE CROSSING. Intersection of a road and a railroad track, or of two railroad tracks.

HELPER. A locomotive added to a train to provide extra power to climb a grade. Called a pusher if it's on the rear of a train.

HIGHBALL. Signal to proceed given by a crew member to an engineer by hand motion, lantern or radio.

HOTBOX. An overheated wheelbox that, if not detected, can burn off and cause a derailment.

IN THE HOLE. On a siding, usually to allow another train to pass.

INCLINE. A railroad that travels up the side of a hill or mountain. An incline follows the shortest possible route from the bottom to the top.

INDUSTRIAL RAILROAD. A railroad owned and operated by an industry to move cars within a factory, plant or mill, and to and from an exchange with a common carrier. In Pennsylvania, industrial railroads are not common carriers.

INTERCHANGE. Junction of two railroads where exchange of cars takes place.

INTERMODAL. Traffic that moves on more than one type of carrier on its journey from shipper to receiver. The most common type of intermodal transport is trucks carried on flatbed railroad cars.

INTERURBAN. An electric railroad (trolley) that runs between cities.

MIXED TRAIN. A train carrying both passengers and freight.

ON THE ADVERTISED. On time.

ON THE GROUND. Derailed.

OPERATING RATIO. The ratio of operating expenses to revenue. A railroad with an operating ratio of 80 or lower is doing well. One with a ratio over 100 may not be in business much longer.

PIGGYBACK. The carrying of truck trailers on railroad cars.

REGIONAL RAILROAD. A railroad bigger than a short line but smaller than a Class 2.

ROAD UNIT. A diesel unit designed for getting trains over the road rather than for switching cars.

ROLLING STOCK. Cars or locomotives.

ROUTE MILE. A mile of railroad line without regard to the number of tracks on that line.

RUNAROUND. A maneuver in which a locomotive is uncoupled, run past the train on another track, and coupled to the other end of that train.

SHORT LINE. A railroad with fewer than 100 miles of main line track.

STEAM RAILROAD. A term still used by regulatory bodies to differentiate ordinary railroads from interurbans and streetcar companies.

SWITCH. A track with movable rails to direct traffic from one track to another (when used as a noun). To sort cars by destination on more than one track (when used as a verb).

SWITCHBACK. An arrangement of track, usually with two switches, used to climb steep grades.

SWITCHING RAILROAD. A railroad whose business is not point-to-point transportation but pickup and delivery for a connecting road.

TRACKAGE RIGHTS. Rights granted by Railroad A to Railroad B to operate on the tracks of Railroad A, usually for a fee and usually with the tenant's crews and locomotives.

UNIT TRAIN. A train carrying a single bulk commodity, usually coal or grain, without any switching en route.

VARNISH. A slang term for a passenger train, derived from the coats of varnish applied to wooden passenger cars.

WYE. An arrangement of tracks forming the letter Y, used for turning cars and engines.

GUIDE TO
Pennsylvania's
TOURIST RAILROADS

DOUBLE BEDROOMS--"B" TYPE
For 1 or 2 Persons

Shown below is sketch of two adjoining Double Bedrooms—"B" Type—one prepared for daytime occupancy, the other for night-time service. Many changes have been incorporated in these new bedrooms. Slight differences as to location of beds and type of furniture prevail in the two rooms. Each may be sold separately or both combined and sold en suite. Both have been re-designed and modernized to provide more comfort, greater convenience for sleeping car passengers. Red lines pin-point outstanding features.

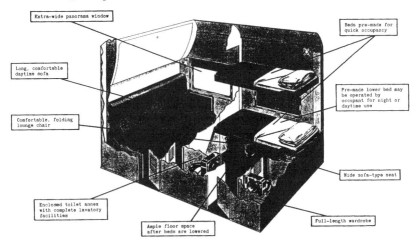

Extra-wide panorama window

Beds pre-made for quick occupancy

Long, comfortable daytime sofa

Pre-made lower bed may be operated by occupant for night or daytime use

Comfortable, folding lounge chair

Wide sofa-type seat

Enclosed toilet annex with complete lavatory facilities

Ample floor space after beds are lowered

Full-length wardrobe

DOUBLE BEDROOMS--"B" TYPE
For 1 or 2 Persons

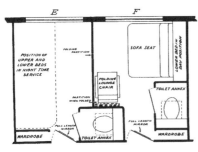

Above sketch shows floor plans of two Double Bedrooms—"B" Type. Each will accommodate 1 or 2 persons and may be sold as separate rooms. Beds in Room E have been placed cross-wise of car. Beds in Room F (adjoining) are positioned parallel to length of car. Passengers may state preference when reserving space. Rooms are so coordinated that by folding back the center partition, the entire facilities of both rooms may be sold en suite as a most attractive Drawing Room accommodating 2, 3 or 4 persons. Dotted lines show arrangement of beds in Room E.

Daytime Features

- Enclosed toilet annex with complete lavatory facilities.
- Extra-wide panorama window allows free, wide-angle vision.
- Long, comfortable daytime sofa in Room E.
- Comfortable lounge chair and sofa-seat in Room F.
- Pre-made lower bed in Room F may be lowered without porter's assistance—day or night.
- Full-length wardrobe provides ample space for clothes.
- Convenient full-length mirrors.

Night-time Features

- Beds are pre-made, thus eliminating inconvenience and affording more privacy en route.
- Beds readied for quick occupancy. Porter will assist in positioning both beds in Room E; upper bed in Room F.
- Ample floor space after beds are lowered.
- Room temperature individually controlled by occupant —night and day.

See Floor Plans 3, 4 and 5, Pages 19 and 20 for location of "B" Type Double Bedrooms in latest type sleeping cars.

Trains in America—
A Brief History

When the first Europeans arrived in North America, they found a land of opportunity and a land of hardship. Travel was especially difficult. Roads were crude, and turned into quagmires when it rained. People and goods moved in horse-drawn carriages and wagons, and to transport large quantities of goods or numbers of people was almost impossible. The railroad was a necessity for the country's economic growth.

Early methods of mass transportation focused on waterways. Rivers and canals were the best ways to move people and goods before the railroad came, but they had limitations, the most serious of which was winter. When the water froze, commerce stopped.

In England, railways were under development. In 1825, the Stockton and Darlington began operations, and the idea quickly moved to the colonies. In 1826, the first railway opened in the United States. The Granite Railroad carried blocks of granite from quarries in Quincy, Massachusetts to docks four miles away. Horses provided the power, and the railroad inspired many others to improve on the idea.

In 1827, Pennsylvania's first railroad opened. The Switchback Railroad in Mauch Chunk (now Jim Thorpe) carried coal from mines to docks on the Lehigh River. Gravity moved the coal cars from the mines down to the river, and mules pulled the cars back up the hill. The mules rode down

43d Year, No. 2   JULY, 1910

THE OFFICIAL GUIDE

OF THE

RAILWAYS

AND

STEAM NAVIGATION LINES

OF THE

UNITED STATES

PORTO RICO

CANADA, MEXICO AND CUBA

ALSO TIME-TABLES OF RAILROADS IN CENTRAL AMERICA

A MONTHLY PERIODICAL PUBLICATION DEVOTED TO THE DISSEMINATION OF PUBLIC INFORMATION
RESPECTING THE STEAM TRANSPORTATION LINES OF THE NORTH AMERICAN CONTINENT;
CHANGES IN TIME AND OFFICIALS, THE CURRENT TIME-TABLES IN EFFECT, MISCELLANEOUS
INFORMATION RELATIVE TO RAILWAY IMPROVEMENTS AND PROGRESS, MAPS, MILEAGE,
LISTS OF STATIONS, CONNECTIONS AND OFFICIALS; OCEAN, COASTWISE AND,
RIVER NAVIGATION ROUTES; AND OTHER ITEMS USEFUL TO THE TRAVELING
PUBLIC, THE BUSINESS COMMUNITY, AND RAILWAY COMPANIES.

ISSUED UNDER THE AUSPICES OF

THE AMERICAN ASSOCIATION OF GENERAL PASSENGER AND TICKET AGENTS

COMPILED AND EDITED UNDER THE DIRECTION OF

W. F. ALLEN, Vice-President and Manager

E. S. ALLEN, Assistant Manager

24 Park Place, New York

THE NATIONAL RAILWAY PUBLICATION COMPANY, PUBLISHERS AND PROPRIETORS

EXECUTIVE OFFICERS:

WM. H. WOOLVERTON, PRESIDENT, 24 PARK PLACE, NEW YORK.

J. B. MOFFITT, Secretary, Room 824, Arcade Building, 15th and Market Streets, Philadelphia, Pa.	FRANK MOONAN, Treasurer, 24 Park Place, New York.

For Sale by Periodical Dealers, News Agents and Booksellers ; also, on Trains, and at the several Railroad
Depots and Ticket Offices in the United States and Canada.

SUBSCRIPTION PRICE, $8.00 PER ANNUM. $1.00 PER COPY.

Courtesy Railroad Museum of Pennsylvania

RAHWAY VALLEY RAILROAD.
(Rahway Valley Company, Lessee.)

June 7, 1909.	Ms	Pas.	Pas.	Pas.	Pas.	Pas.	Pas.	Pas.	Pas.	Sun.	Sun.	Sun.	Sun
		A M	A M	A M	Noon	P M	P M	P M		A M	A M	P M	P M
New York.............lve.													
Liberty Street..(C.R.R. of N.J.)		†600	†715	†815	†100	†230	†500	†830		‡7 30	‡1000	‡230	‡4 30
West 23d Street... "			7 05	8 05	11 50	2 20	4 60	6 20		7 20	9 50	2 29	4 20
Newark (*Broad Street*)......		6 12	6 50	7 55	11 30	2 35	4 32	8 13		7 10	9 55	2 46	3 66
Elizabethport................		6 33	7 43	8 43	11 27	2 58	5 11	6 58		8 07	10 30	3 06	5 02
Elizabeth....................		6 39	7 48	8 48	11 32	3 03	5 36	7 01		8 13	10 36	3 12	5 08
Roselle (Roselle Park).......	0	6 45	7 53	8 53	11 38	3 08	5 42	7 08		8 20	10 43	3 17	5 15
Aldene......................		6 49	7 58	9 04	12 41	3 10	5 46	7 09		8 24	10 45	3 19	5 17
Michigan Avenue............	A M	6 52	8 01	9 10	12 44	3 13	5 48	7 12	A M	8 27	11 48	3 22	5 21
Kenilworth (Central Station)..	†6 00	6 55	8 04	9 13	12 47	3 16	5 61	7 15	‡7 15	8 30	10 50	3 26	5 24
Kenilworth (Warren Street)..	2.4	6 02	6 57	8 06	9 15	12 49	5 18	5 63	7 17	7 17	8 33	10 52	3 27	5 26
Union......................	3.4	6 04	6 59	8 08	9 17	12 51	3 20	6 55	7 19	7 19	8 35	10 55	3 30	5 28
Arion......................	4.4	6 06	7 01	8 10	9 19	12 53	3 22	5 57	7 21	7 21	8 38	10 57	3 53	5 31
Springfield.................	5.8	6 08	7 04	8 12	9 21	12 55	3 24	5 59	7 23	7 23	8 41	10 59	3 36	5 34
Baltusrol..................	6.8	6 10	7 06	8 15	9 24	12 57	3 28	5 61	7 26	7 25	8 44	11 01	3 39	5 37
Summit....................	8.8	6 16	7 12	8 20	9 31	1 03	3 31	6 08	7 30	7 30	8 49	11 06	3 46	5 42
[ARRIVE		A M	A M	A M	A M	P M	P M	P M	P M	A M	A M	A M	A M

STATIONS.	Mls	Pas.	Pas.	Pas.	Pas.	Pas.	Pas.	Pas.	Pas.	Sun.	Sun.	Sun.	Sun.
[LEAVE		A M	A M	A M	A M	P M	P M	P M	P M	A M	A M	P M	P M
Summit....................	0	†6 25	†7 33	†8 33	†1050	†2 48	†5 10	†6 55	‡7 50	‡9 41	§11 55	§4 50	§8 00
Baltusrol..................	2.0	6 30	7 38	8 38	10 55	2 45	5 19	5 40	7 56	9 46	1 41	4 56	8 05
Springfield.................	3.0	6 32	7 40	8 40	10 57	2 47	5 18	6 42	7 58	9 48	1 43	4 58	6 07
Arion......................	4.4	6 34	7 42	8 42	10 59	2 58	5 20	6 44	8 01	9 51	1 45	4 44	6 09
Union......................	5.4	6 36	7 44	8 44	11 01	2 52	5 22	6 46	8 04	9 53	1 48	4 44	6 11
Kenilworth (Warren Street)..	6.4	6 38	7 46	8 46	11 03	2 54	5 24	6 48	8 06	9 54	1 50	4 48	8 15
Kenilworth (Central Station)..		6 39	7 48	8 48	11 05	2 55	5 28	6 50	8 08	9 55	1 52	4 48	8 15
Michigan Avenue............		6 42	7 51	8 51	11 08	2 58	5 29	6 53	8 11	9 59	1 56	4 51	8 18
Aldene......................		6 48	8 05	9 03	12 14	3 03	5 34	7 06	8 16	10 04	2 01	4 67	6 24
Roselle (Roselle Park).......	8.8	6 51	8 09	9 07	11 18	3 08	5 44	7 09	8 20	10 08	2 05	4 63	6 27
Elizabeth..................		6 58	8 15	9 12	11 23	3 14	5 51	7 15	8 27	10 15	2 18	5 18	8 35
Elizabethport...............		7 07	8 27	9 44	11 28	3 20	5 69	7 20	8 33	10 21	2 18	5 15	8 41
Newark (*Broad Street*)......		7 26	8 40	9 47	12 46	4 14	"	"	"	11 18	2 36	6 02	"
West 23d St.(C.R.R. of N.Y.)		7 40	8 57	10 10	12 01	4 18	7 16	8 10	9 20	11 10	3 10	8 18	7 10
Liberty Street.... "		7 30	8 47	9 45	12 00	3 55	6 52	7 55	9 10	11 00	3 55	6 55	7 20
New York.............arr.		A M	A M	A M	P M	P M	P M	P M	P M	A M	P M	P M	P M

C. J. WITTENBERG, President,
11 Broadway, New York.

E. G. THOMPSON, Vice-Prest.,
29 Broadway, New York.

JAMES S. GILBERT, Treas.,
200 Fifth Avenue, New York.

H. F. DANKEL, Gen. Mgr.,
Kenilworth, N.J.

† Daily, except Sunday.
‡ Sunday only.
Eastern time.

This railroad has direct connection and does general business with the Lehigh Valley R.R., Central R.R. of New Jersey, Baltimore & Ohio R.R. and Philadelphia & Reading R.R., and has under construction connection with the Delaware, Lackawanna & Western R.R. It provides extensive shipping facilities for the towns lying between the Orange Mountains and above railroads, and particularly for the manufacturing town of Kenilworth, where many New York manufacturers are located.

EAST BROAD TOP RAILROAD & COAL CO.

R. S. SHIBERT, Prest. & Gen. Mgr., Orbisonia, Pa.
EDWARD ROBERTS, Vice-Prest., Lafayette Bldg.,5th & Chestnut Sts., Phila., Pa.
S. J. LIVINGSTON, Sec'y & Treas., "
C. D. JONES, Aud. and Asst. to Prest. and Gen. Mgr.,Orbisonia, Pa.

BYRON E. WOODCOCK, Chf. Eng'r, Orbisonia, Pa.
T. R. SHANKS, Master Mechanic, Orbisonia, Pa.
J. G. MURPHY, Roadmaster, "
J. N. STEVENS, Foreman, Bridges and Buildings, Orbisonia, Pa.

4	2	Ms.	June 27, 1910.	1	3
A M	P M		[LEAVE	ARRIVE	P M
1025	4 25	11 35	........Philadelphia......	6 20	8 40
Noon			[LEAVE	ARRIVE	P M
1201	3 00		........Pittsburg......	2 10	6 28

4	2	Ms.		1	3
A M	A M	P M	[LEAVE	ARRIVE	
†445	†1215	†9 55	0	....Mount Union[1]...	
5 03	11 33	10 14	4.0	.....Aughwick.....	9 00
5 15	11 45	10 25	7.0	.....Shirley......	8 50
5 30	12 01	10 40	A 11.0	arr.....Orbisonia..lve.	8 35
5 40	1 30	10 45	‡330	11.0	lve.....Orbisonia..arr.	8 40
6 50	1 40	12 01	5 41	14.0	.....Pogue......	8 07
8 00	1 66	12 13	5 56	17.0	...Three Springs...	7 55
6 09	2 10	12 23	6 00	19.0	.....Saltillo......	7 45
6 38	2 41	11 55	6 30	24.0	.....Cole's......	7 20
6 45	2 52	12 02	6 37	25.0	...Rocky Ridge...	7 15
			25.6	.....Wrays Hill.....	
			26.0	.....Martins.....	
8 51	2 58	12 10	6 45	27.0	.....Cook's......	7 08
7 00	3 10	11 20	7 00	30.0	...Robertsdale...	†700
P M	P M	Noon	P M			[LEAVE

Daily, except Sunday. Eastern time.

Connections.—[1] With P. R. R.

SHADE GAP BRANCH.

No. 12	No. 10	Mls	June 27, 1910.	Mls	No. 9	No. 11
†6 40 P M	†6 55 A M	0	lve.....Orbisonia....arr.	10	8 25 A M	7 00 P M
5 46 "	7 02 "	2	.....Blacklog.....	8	8 18 "	6 55 "
5 51 "	7 06 "	4	...Cedar Rock...	6	8 10 "	6 48 "
5 54 "	7 09 "	5	..Locke Valley..	5	8 06 "	6 45 "
6 00 "	7 15 "	6	...Shade Gap[2]..	4	8 00 "	6 40 "
8 15 P M	7 30 A M	10	.....Neelyton..lve.	0	7 45 A M	†6 25 P M

GEORGES VALLEY RAILROAD.
J. LOVEJOY, Superintendent, Union, Me.
Trains leave **Union**[1] for **Warren**[2] (8 miles) †7 40 a.m., †1 25 p.m. Returning, leave Warren †10 20 a.m., †4 25 p.m. Running time 30 minutes.
† Daily, except Sunday. *February*, 1910.
Connections.—[1] With stages for Appleton, Searsmont, East Union, and South Hope. [2] With Maine Central R.R. *Eastern time.*

PHILIPSBURG RAILWAY & QUARRY CO.
HENRY BROWN, Resident Manager, Philipsburg, Que.
From **Stanbridge**[1] to Philipsburg (9 miles). No passenger service during Winter months. *April*, 1908.
Connections.—[1] With Canadian Pacific and Central Vermont Rys.

LAUREL & TALLAHOMA WESTERN RAILWAY.
P. S. GARDINER, General Manager, Laurel, Miss.
Logging road, connecting at Laurel, Miss., with Gulf & Ship Island R.R. New Orleans & North-eastern Ry. to New Orleans, Mobile & Chicago Ry. Operates about 60 miles. *February*, 1910.

THE ASHLAND & WESTERN RAILWAY CO.
J. RAMSEY, JR., President. F. A. WALSH, Aud. & Asst. Treas.
N. P. RAMSEY, Vice-Prest. & Gen. Mgr. | JOHN DORSEY, Gen. Fht. & Pas. Agt.
General Office—Ashland, Ohio.
The railway connecting Ashland, O., with Pennsylvania System.

No. 3	No. 1	Mls	November 8, 1909.	No. 2	No. 4
†4 50 P M	†9 00 A M	0	lve.....Ashland[1]..arr.	12 50 Noon	8 00 P M
5 09 "	"		......England.....	12 38 "	7 48 "
5 15 "	9 45 "	11.1	....Jeromeville...	12 25 "	7 35 "
5 23 "	9 53 "	14.5	.....Sprengs.....	12 17 "	7 27 "
5 36 "	10 05 "	19.6	.......Funk......	12 05 Noon	7 15 "
5 40 "	10 16 "	20.1	.....Horace.....	11 57 A M	7 12 "
5 50 "	10 22 "	21.0	.....Craigos.....	11 52 "	7 01 "
6 00 P M	10 30 A M	23.0	arr.....Custaloga[2]..lve.	11 40 A M	†6 50 P M
			(*Penna. Co. Junction.*)		
			(*Via Penna. Co.*)		
7 00 P M	11 28 A M		arr......Shreve.....lve.	10 49 A M	6 15 P M
7 07 "	11 34 A M		arr......Wooster..lve.	10 36 A M	6 58 P M
7 35 P M	12 03 Noon		arr......Orrville.....lve.	10 14 A M	†5 50 P M
6 40 P M	11 13 A M		arr.....Loudonville...lve.	†1053 A M	†8 25 P M

Ashland & Western trains await arrival of Pennsylvania trains, thus insuring a connection. *Central time.*

Connections.—[1] With Erie R.R. [2] With Pennsylvania Co.

WHARTON & NORTHERN RAILWAY.
EDWARD KELLY, General Superintendent, Wharton, N.J.
Trains leave **Wharton**[1] for **Green Pond Junction**[2] †7 20 a.m., a2 50 p.m.; for Green Lake †6 05, †9 20, ‡10 45 a.m., ‡1 35, a260, †5 55 p.m.; for Oreland †6 55 p.m.; for Lake Denmark †7 33 a.m. Leave Green Pond Junction ‡11 10 a.m., ‡1 40, †3 50 p.m., arrives Wharton †2 48 noon. Leave Green Lake †6 45, ‡11 40, ‡12 50 a.m., †1 50, †4 10, ‡6 55, †6 30 p.m., arrive Wharton †7 15 a.m., ‡2 38, 12 26 noon, 2 35, 4 68, 6 25, 7 25 p.m. Leaves Lake Denmark †8 00 a.m., arrives Wharton 8 25 a.m. Leaves Oreland †8 48 p.m., arrives Wharton 7 25 p.m. *June 25*, 1910.
† Daily, except Sunday; ‡ Sunday only; a Tuesday, Thursday and Saturday; b Tuesday and Thursday; § Saturday only. *Eastern time.*
Connections.—[1] With Central R.R. of New Jersey and Delaware, Lackawanna & Western R.R. [2] With N.Y. Susquehanna & West. R.R.

BIG FALLS RAILWAY.
J. H. WALL, President, Oshkosh, Wis.
Extends from **Hunting**[1] to Big Falls and Norske (21 miles). Train leaves Hunting †10 30 a.m., arriving Big Falls 11 30 a.m. Leaves Big Falls †7 45 a.m., arrives Hunting 8 50 a.m. Irregular service Big Falls to Norske. *April*, 1908.
† Daily, except Sunday.
Connection.—[1] With Chicago & North-Western Ry.

MARION & RYE VALLEY RAILWAY.
VIRGINIA-SOUTHERN RAILROAD.
H. B. JEFFREY, Secretary, Auditor, Freight and Pas. Agent, Marion, Va.
Train leaves **Marion**[1] †8 00 a.m., arrives **Sugar Grove**[2] (18 miles) 9 45 a.m., arrives Fairwood (30 miles) 11 30 a.m., arrives Fairwood (30 miles) 11 30 a.m., arrive Sugar Grove 2 56 p.m. Leaves Sugar Grove †2 38 p.m., arrives Marion 4 16 p.m. m.
† Daily, except Sunday. *January* 11, 1909.
Connections.—[1] With Norfolk & Western Ry. [2] Junction Virginia-Southern R.R. and Marion & Rye Valley Ry.

the inclines on sliding platforms, and legend says that they enjoyed the rides so much that they refused to walk down the slopes.

In 1829, the era of steam locomotives in the United States began. In May, the Stourbridge Lion came from England and arrived in New York. The locomotive got its name because it came from the city of Stourbridge, England, and it had a bright red lion's head painted on the boiler.

From New York, the locomotive traveled by water to Honesdale, Pennsylvania. On August 9, with a man named Horatio Allen at the throttle, the Lion made its maiden voyage. The train traveled about three miles on a track made of hemlock stringers and iron bars. The Lion proved itself worthy, but the track was inadequate, and the Lion's reign in Honesdale was brief. Nevertheless, the Lion began the era of steam locomotives in the United States.

Soon, men were working on railroads up and down the East Coast. The first regular passenger railway in America to employ steam locomotives was the Charleston and Hamburg in South Carolina. It was running in December, 1830.

Building railroads along the coast was comparatively easy. The mountains presented a bigger challenge, and the mountains aren't far inland. The first railroad built across the Allegheny Mountains was the Portage Road, a complicated system in central Pennsylvania that used inclined planes to lift rail cars over the mountains. The Portage Road was 36 miles long, complex, and slow, but it worked.

The opening of Horseshoe Curve in 1854 doesn't draw as much attention as the completion of the transcontinental railroad in 1869, but the Curve was just as important. By conquering the Alleghenies, the Curve opened up the West and made the Pennsylvania Railroad one of the biggest and most powerful companies in the world.

Through the rest of the 19th century, railroads moved into every big city and almost every small town. The rail depot became the center of the town's economic and social activity as trains made it possible to do business with people far away and to cross the country in a week. Locomotives became more powerful and faster, and designers incorporated creature comforts into passenger cars. The train eventually became a hotel and a restaurant on steel wheels.

Today, passenger train travel has almost vanished from the American scene, but trains still have an appeal, so tourist trains are running to give people the enjoyment of riding a train. Tourist trains may seem like a fairly modern idea, but they've actually been a part of railroad life almost since the first train operated. For people whose only form of transportation was a horse-drawn buggy, a ride on a train was quite a thrill, even if they didn't have anywhere to go.

The following chapters describe some of the train-riding thrills available today in Pennsylvania. They'll also tell you how to get there, the best places to take pictures of the trains, and what else there is to see—train-related or otherwise—nearby.

Southeast Region

Gettysburg—Gettysburg Scenic Rail Tours

Telephone: 717-334-6932

Location and Directions: Gettysburg is in south-central Pennsylvania, at the junction of U.S. routes 30 and 15. The station is at 106 N. Washington St., right in the center of town. From the north or south, take Route 15 and go west on Route 30. Washington Street is one block west of Lincoln Square, and the station is one block north of Route 30.

Now and Then: The Gettysburg Railroad is both a freight and a tourist railroad. It's been in operation under different names since the 1860s.

The Station: The old depot has a ticket booth, a waiting room, and a souvenir shop.

The Route: The regular ride begins on the north side of Gettysburg and travels north to Biglerville, about eight miles away. A 50-mile round trip, which operates on selected Saturdays and for Fall Foliage, goes north to Mount Holly Springs.

Approximate Trip Time: One and a half hours

The Ride: The station is on the northern edge of downtown Gettysburg. As the train leaves the station, it passes through a small rail yard and past Gettysburg College. Just beyond the college, the train enters the battlefield where the most famous battle of the Civil War occurred. Most of the battlefield is actually

41

Gettysburg Scenic Rail Tours.

The double decker, a former auto carrier, can seat 240 passengers.

on the south side of town, but from the train you can view some monuments and fields where first-day (July 1, 1863) skirmishes took place.

The train passes through a small wooded area and then enters farm country, rumbling through back yards and tiny villages as it winds its way to Biglerville. There, the freight operation of the railroad serves several businesses, including Musselman's, which makes a variety of apple products. At Biglerville, the train stops and the engine moves from the north end of the consist to the south end for the return trip to Gettysburg. On the 50-mile rides, the character of the land changes from farmland to woodland as the terrain becomes more hilly north of Biglerville.

The Region: "Fourscore and seven years ago our fathers brought forth on this continent a new nation, conceived in liberty and dedicated to the proposition that all men are created equal." Those words began Abraham Lincoln's Gettysburg Address. Four and a half months before he delivered it, the event that inspired it raged through the streets and fields of Gettysburg.

No place in America has a closer association with a single event than this small town in south-central Pennsylvania. From July 1 to July 3, 1863, the bloodiest battle of the Civil War stamped Gettysburg with an eternal identity. On November 19 of that year, Abraham Lincoln delivered his Gettysburg Address, and since then Gettysburg's fame has come from that single battle.

Today, the battle still dominates daily life in Gettysburg. The Gettysburg National Military Park covers more than five square miles, and it's especially beautiful in April and May when the dogwoods bloom. Millions of visitors come every year, and scores of businesses ring the battlefield.

The battlefield is so big that exploring all of it on foot is difficult. A marked automobile route is 17 miles long; bicycle tours are available nearby, and bus tours are widely advertised.

Beyond the battlefield, Adams County is a productive

agricultural region that's the biggest fruit-growing county in Pennsylvania. Most of the orchards are near Biglerville, which is about eight miles north of Gettysburg. The orchards are especially beautiful in late April and early May when thousands of apple, peach, cherry, and plum trees are in bloom.

Picture Taking: This line roughly parallels PA Route 34 for its entire route. It crosses Route 34 about halfway between Gettysburg and Biglerville, just south of Goldenville Road.

Schedule: The basic season is April through October, with Christmas specials.

April—Saturday, Sunday: 1, 3 P.M.

May, June—Thursday, Friday: 10 A.M., 12:30 P.M.; Saturday, Sunday: 1, 3 P.M.

July, August—Monday to Friday: 11 A.M., 1 P.M.; Saturday, Sunday: 11 A.M., 1, 3 P.M.

September, October—Labor Day, Thursday, Friday: 11 A.M., 1 P.M.; Saturday, Sunday: 11 A.M., 1, 3 P.M.

Fall Foliage 50-mile rides—first three weekends in October: 10 A.M.

Special Events:

Easter Bunny Train—first Sunday in April: 1, 3 P.M.

Civil War Train Raid—July 4, 5: 11 A.M., 1:30 P.M.

Lincoln Train—first weekend in August: 1, 3 P.M.

Civil War Train Raid—third weekend in September: 1, 3:30 P.M.

Halloween Train—last weekend in October: 1, 3 P.M.

Christmas Train—first two weekends in December: 1, 3 P.M.

Apple Blossom Dinner Trip (50 miles)—first Saturday in May: 2 P.M.

Summer's Eve Dinner Trip (50 miles)—Friday before summer solstice: 6 P.M.

Hobo Special (50 miles)—third Saturday in July: 5 P.M.

Moonlight Dinner Trip (50 miles)—third Friday in August: 6 P.M.

Fall Harvest Dinner Trip (50 miles)—last Saturday in September: 2 P.M.

Fall Foliage (50 miles)—first three Saturdays, second and third Sundays of October: 10 A.M.

Fares: Regular
Adults $8.00
Seniors (65 and up) $7.50
Children 3 to 12 $4.00
          Special Events
Adults $9.00
Seniors (65 and up) $8.50
Children 3 to 12 $5.00
          Special 50-Mile Trips
Adults $18.00
Seniors (65 and up) $16.00
Children 3 to 12 $10.00

Power: Steam and diesel

Nearby Attractions: Gettysburg Battlefield; Biglerville orchards; the National Apple Museum, at 154 W. Hanover St. in Biglerville, which tells the history of apples and apple products (call 717-677-4556 for operating hours)

Tourist Information: Gettysburg Convention and Visitors Bureau, 35 Carlisle St., Gettysburg, PA 17325, telephone 717-334-6274

Nearest Tourist Railroad: Northern Central—45 miles away

Kempton—Wanamaker, Kempton & Southern Railroad

Telephone: 610-756-6469

Location and Directions: The W, K & S is in northern Berks County, far from any beaten path, in the small town of Kempton. PA routes 143 and 737 run through Kempton. The nearest cities are Reading to the south and Allentown to the east. To get to Kempton, take PA 143 or PA 737 North from U.S. 22/I-78 and look for the signs to Kempton.

Now and Then: The W, K & S is now strictly a tourist railroad. Previously, it was a Reading branch line. Freight service ended in 1962.

The Station: The W, K & S operates out of the old Kempton station, which has a ticket booth, a snack bar, and a souvenir shop.

The steam engine on the Wanamaker, Kempton & Southern does its runaround in the village of Wanamakers.

Wanamaker, Kempton & Southern Railroad.

The Route: The W, K & S runs north for about 6.5 miles from Kempton in Berks County to Wanamakers in Lehigh County. For some of the route, the train runs parallel to PA Route 143.

Approximate Trip Time: Under one hour

The Ride: Unlike many other tourist lines, the W, K & S does not do any freight service since it connects neither with water nor further rail transport at either end of the line.

As the steam engine comes to life, the train lurches out of the old station. If you're in the open car, you'll notice cinders flying from the engine and landing all around you. The train gains speed, but not too much.

As the train leaves the station, you'll see the railroad's repair facilities on your right. Next comes the tiny village of Trexler, which features an old log home erected in 1734. Once it was the village inn, and if you look closely you can see irregular marks on its porch. These came from harvesters who drove their sickles into the wall before going inside.

The railroad runs beside Ontelaunee Creek, which is a major water supply for the Reading area. At this stage, the train is going uphill, and you can feel the engine working hard. Soon the train comes to Furhman's Grove, a picnic area where you can get off and wait for the next train.

After a long curve, the line crosses the Ontelaunee Creek and enters Lehigh County. Soon the train enters the village of Wanamakers, beside PA Route 143. To the left is the Blue Mountain range, with Hawk Mountain particularly noticeable as you travel by. The train stops in Wanamakers for the engine to move from one end of the train to the other. On Sundays, the old Wanamakers train station is open as an antique shop.

The Region: Kempton itself is a very small village with several restaurants and businesses. The surrounding region is rural, and the train tickets make humorous reference to the region's predominant characteristic with such "Regulations" as

• Conductors are permitted to accept tickets only—no produce or I.O.U.'s

• Passengers, if needed, will assist train crew in pushing train, removing livestock and fallen trees from track, and in other assorted calamities

• Watch out for card sharks

The biggest attraction nearby is Hawk Mountain Sanctuary, the nation's first sanctuary for birds of prey. During the spring and autumn migratory seasons, thousands of raptors (such as hawks, eagles, and ospreys) follow the prevailing winds over the mountain peaks. At any time of year, the top of the mountain provides great views of the valley below. A visitors center contains displays and a museum.

Picture Taking: PA Route 143 north of Kempton

Schedule: The basic season is May through October, with Christmas specials.

Steam Train

May, June, September—Sunday: 1, 2, 3, 4 P.M.

July, August, October—Saturday, Sunday: 1, 2, 3, 4 P.M.

Holidays—Memorial Day, July 4, Labor Day: 1, 2, 3, 4 P.M.

Diesel Train

June, September—First and third Saturdays: 1, 2, 3, 4 P.M.

Special Events: Mother's Day Special, Sandman Special (late June, in conjunction with the Kempton Fair), Kids' Fun Weekend (first Saturday and Sunday in August), Harvest Moon Special (last weekend in September), Halloween Train, Santa Claus Special

Fares: Adults are $4.50 and children (3 to 11) are $2.50.

Power: Steam and diesel

Nearby Attractions: Hawk Mountain; Lehigh County Velodrome; the Pennsylvania Dutch Folk and Culture Center at Lehnartsville; Roadside America at Shartlesville, a large indoor miniature village with a big model train display (See Museums chapter)

Tourist Information: Reading and Berks County Visitors Bureau, P.O. Box 6627, Reading, PA 19610, telephone 800-443-6610; or, Lehigh Valley Convention and Visitors Bureau, P.O. Box 20785, Lehigh Valley, PA 18002-0785, telephone 800-747-0561

Nearest Tourist Railroad: East Penn—17 miles away

Kutztown—East Penn Railway

Telephone: 610-683-9202

Location and Directions: Kutztown is in northern Berks County, between Reading and Allentown on U.S. Route 222. The station is at the intersection of Railroad and Main streets. To get there, take 222 to the outskirts of Kutztown, and then follow Main Street through town. Route 222 goes around the town, so look for Main Street.

Now and Then: The East Penn is strictly a tourist operation. The original route, built in 1857, was the Allentown and Auburn Railroad.

The Station: The East Penn has a beautiful depot with a ticket booth, snack bar, and souvenir shop.

The Route: The East Penn Railroad runs basically east from the small town of Kutztown to the smaller town of Topton.

Approximate Trip Time: One hour

The Ride: The trip begins in the college town of Kutztown and rolls slowly through the scenic farmlands of Pennsylvania Dutch Country. Along the route, the train passes fields, houses, and quarries. Throughout southeastern Pennsylvania are large limestone deposits, which make the soil fertile and the region good for quarrying.

The train runs from Kutztown to Topton, and at Topton a Conrail line from Reading to Allentown parallels the tracks of the East Penn.

The Region: Kutztown is in the heart of Pennsylvania Dutch Country, a region with no definite boundaries where Mennonite and Amish farmers work the land and where their culture, with German roots, is prevalent. "Pennsylvania Dutch" refers both to the people and the language, which is a combination of English and German. Almost all of its speakers live in this area. They are not Dutch; the word is a distortion of "Deutsch"—the German word for "German."

In Kutztown, antiques are big business. Renninger's Antique and Farmers' Market at 740 Noble St. is open on weekends and attracts hundreds of dealers.

East Penn Railway.

The little green locomotive is ready to pull the train to Topton.

Picture Taking: At the station

Schedule: The basic schedule is Saturdays and Sundays from June through the end of the year at 12 noon and 2 P.M.

Special Events:

Bunny Express—Saturday and Sunday of the weekend before Easter, and the Saturday just before Easter

Weekday school trips—April, May

Father's Day—June

Pennsylvania German Festival—last weekend in June and first in July

Old Time Railroad Days—last weekend in August

Fares:

Adults	$8.00
Seniors (65 and up)	$7.00
Children 2 to 12	$4.00

Power: Diesel

Nearby Attractions: Crystal Cave; Kutztown Pennsylvania German Festival; Reading Outlet Center; Maple Grove Raceway (cars); Renninger's Antique Market; Rodale Institute Experimental Farm; Reading Phillies (AA)

Tourist Information: Reading and Berks County Visitors Bureau, P.O. Box 6627, Reading, PA 19610, telephone 800-443-6610

Nearest Tourist Railroad: Wanamaker, Kempton & Southern—17 miles away

Middletown—Middletown & Hummelstown Railroad

Telephone: 717-944-4435

Location and Directions: Middletown is about 10 miles south of Harrisburg, along the Susquehanna River. The M & H Station is at 136 Brown St.. From Harrisburg, go east on PA 283. Exit at the Middletown & Hummelstown ramp and follow the sign to Middletown. That road becomes Vine Street. Go west on Main Street (PA 230) and quickly left on Race Street. The

Middletown & Hummelstown Railroad.

The M & H has the nickname "the Milk & Honey Line."

station is at Race and Mill streets. From the south, come into Middletown on PA 441, which becomes Union Street. Turn right on Mill Street and proceed to the station.

Now and Then: The M & H is both a freight and a tourist line. The original M & H began operations in 1890. From then until 1976, it was a Reading branch.

The Station: The M & H has a station but doesn't use it for passenger operations. Passengers purchase tickets at a booth adjacent to the line.

The Route: The M & H begins its run in downtown Middletown and then runs parallel to the Swatara Creek for about five miles before it crosses the creek at Indian Echo Cavern.

Approximate Trip Time: One and a quarter hours

The Ride: The M & H is a working freight line, and its biggest customers are chemical companies. They're on the right side of the train as it heads out of the station. After the first industrial-looking mile, the line assumes a wooded character as it travels beside the Swatara Creek and through the back yards of some homes. This isn't a mountainous region, but the train does climb a 2.92 percent grade, which is much steeper than most lines encounter, and the engine works hard to move the train over the hill. On busy days, the line uses two diesel engines to pull four or more passenger cars.

From 1827 to 1884, the Union Canal operated along this route, and many parts of the canal are still visible. You can still see Canal Lock #33, as well as lime kilns which converted limestone into lime and Horse Thief Cave where, according to legend, horse thieves hid their stolen steeds. Near the end of the ride, the line crosses the Swatara on a bridge that's about 35 feet above the water. The train then stops and changes direction at Indian Echo Caverns where passengers may disembark and take a 45-minute cavern tour.

On the return trip, the train comes alive as a banjo player or an accordion player leads passengers in singing railroad songs and doing the "Chicken Dance" in the aisles.

Back at the station, visitors may take an escorted tour through the train yard each operating day at 12 :15 P.M.

The Region: Middletown gained fame (or infamy) in 1979 when a nuclear reactor at Three Mile Island threatened to melt down. That reactor is closed, but its twin is still operating at the plant, which is south of Middletown along PA Route 441. Three Mile Island is actually in the middle of the Susquehanna River, and it's closed to visitors, but a visitor center on Route 441 tells the story of the accident.

The biggest tourist attraction nearby is Hershey, known as Chocolate Town USA. In Hershey, many of America's favorite candy bars take shape, and Chocolate World shows how the process works. In summer, HersheyPark delights visitors with its amusement rides and entertainment.

Upstream from Middletown is Harrisburg, the capital of Pennsylvania. The state capitol is open to visitors, and City Island offers many recreational opportunities. The Harrisburg Senators AA baseball team is one of the few teams that play in the middle of a river, and the *Pride of the Susquehanna* is a paddle wheeler that plies the waters of the river.

Picture Taking: On Route 230 east of Middletown

Schedule: The basic season is May through October, with special runs every month except January.

May—starting on Memorial Day weekend, Saturday, Sunday, Monday: 11 A.M., 1, 2:30, 4 P.M.

June—Saturday, Sunday: 11 A.M., 1, 2:30, 4 P.M.

July, August—Tuesday through Friday: 11 A.M., 1, 2:30 P.M.; Saturday, Sunday: 11 A.M., 1, 2:30, 4 P.M.

September—Sunday, Labor Day: 11 A.M., 1, 2:30, 4 P.M.

October—Saturday, Sunday: 11 A.M., 1, 2:30, 4 P.M.

Note: All trains depart Indian Echo Caverns 40 minutes after dcparting Middletown.

Special Events: Easter, Fall Foliage, Christmas Rides, New Year's Eve. Dinner Trains: Valentine's Day (February), Mother's Day (May), Father's Day (June), M & H anniversary (early August), Late Summer Odyssey (late August), Summer

Farewell (late September), Fall Harvest (mid-October)

Fares: Regular

Adults	$7.00
Children 3 to 11	$3.00

Group Rates
(20 or more paying passengers)

Adult	$6.00
Children 3 to 11	$2.70

Dinner Trains

Adults	$28.50
Children	$20.00

Power: Diesel

Nearby Attractions: Hershey, including HersheyPark and the chocolate factory; Three Mile Island; Harrisburg and the state capitol

Tourist Information: Harrisburg, Hershey, Carlisle Tourism and Convention Bureau, 114 Walnut St., Harrisburg 17108-0969, telephone 800-995-0969, web site http://hhc.welcome.com

Nearest Tourist Railroad: Strasburg—39 miles away

New Freedom—Northern Central Railway

Telephone and Web Site: 800-94-TRAIN or 717-235-4000; http://www.classicrail.com/ncry

Location and Directions: New Freedom is in southern York County, about 3.5 miles west of I-83. From 83, take PA 851 to New Freedom. Turn right on Penn Street, and the station is straight ahead.

Now and Then: The Northern Central is currently just a tourist railroad, but its operators are hoping to return freight service. The Northern Central was one of the earliest railroads in the country, chartered in 1828. On his way to Gettysburg to deliver his Address in 1863, Abraham Lincoln rode on the Northern Central. Hurricane Agnes in 1972 washed out many bridges and effectively killed the Northern Central.

The Station: The Northern Central began in 1996, operating

Northern Central Railway. (Courtesy Northern Central Railway)

A powerful B & O (Baltimore & Ohio) locomotive provides the power for the Northern Central Railway.

out of several rail cars parked near the New Freedom station. A project to restore the old station is underway and funds are being raised for the effort.

The Route: The Northern Central shares the rail corridor with a rail trail that runs north from New Freedom to Seven Valleys. The line once had two tracks; now it has only one, and the other right-of-way has been converted into a trail.

Approximate Trip Time: Two hours

The Ride: The Northern Central's approach is unique among Pennsylvania's tourist railroads. While the other lines focus on the ride itself, the Northern Central focuses on dining and entertainment. With its modern (1950s) passenger cars and powerful Streamliner diesel engine, the Northern Central provides a smooth and comfortable ride through a scenic wooded and agricultural area.

This line is also unique in Pennsylvania because it shares the right-of-way with a hiking and biking trail, and the train makes five stops along the route. Hikers and bikers can ride the train in one direction and return under their own power.

The line hugs a little creek for much of its route, and in the wooded areas many forms of wildlife make their homes. Deer, herons, and egrets are frequently visible from the train window, as are walkers and bicyclists on the adjacent trail. The region is rather hilly, and the line travels through one short tunnel.

On board, the wait staff provides excellent service, and the train cars offer private dining compartments and opportunities for group outings.

The Region: New Freedom is in southern York County, about 35 miles north of Baltimore. The region is rural with small towns like New Freedom scattered among rich, rolling farmlands. Adjacent to the train station are several restaurants and a bike shop.

York is a historic colonial city that was the first capital of the United States and home to the Continental Congress from September 1777 to June 1778. Today, York is a city of manufacturing whose most famous names are Harley Davidson,

Caterpillar, and York Barbell. Local farmers bring their wares to the downtown York Market on Tuesday, Thursday, and Saturday. The most famous event in York is the York Fair, America's oldest fair, which takes place in mid-September.

Picture Taking: All along the route on the adjacent hiking trail

Schedule: This line has a rather flexible schedule. The basic schedule is weekends all year, with occasional weekday specials. However, the days of operation and the times of departure change from week to week, and on many weekends the dinner and entertainment specials operate either on Friday and Saturday or on Saturday and Sunday. The Trailsider Service for bikers and hikers, a ticket to ride without eating, traveling on a separate car but on the regular train, operates on weekends in spring, summer, and fall.

To learn the full schedule for the Northern Central, call ahead for information.

Special Events: Every excursion is a special event on the Northern Central. The owner's philosophy is to use his train as a moving setting for dining and entertainment. He uses a wide variety of themes for the Northern Central's rides, tying in with holidays and events whenever possible. Some of the themes used in 1997 were a World War II USO Troop Train (Memorial Day), Secretary's Day Lunch, 50s Party, 60s Party, Hawaiian Night, and Father's Day Dinner.

Fares: The fares for dinner and entertainment rides range from $14.99 for the party trains to $99.99 for New Year's Eve. The most common prices are $34.99, $39.99, and $49.99. The Trailsider costs $5.00 for a one-way ticket, $3.00 for the bicycle rack fee, and $9.00 for an all day multi-trip ticket.

Power: Diesel

Nearby Attractions: Adjacent rail trail; Harley Davidson Museum in York; Baltimore

Tourist Information: York County Convention and Visitors Bureau, 1 Market Way E., York, PA 17405, telephone 800-673-2429, web site http://yrkpa.kias.com

Nearest Tourist Railroad: Stewartstown—eight miles away

New Hope—New Hope & Ivyland Railroad

Telephone: 215-598-0890

Location and Directions: New Hope is on the Delaware River, about 30 miles northeast of Philadelphia and 60 miles southwest of New York. To reach the station, take exit 27 of the Pennsylvania Turnpike. Go north on PA 611 to U.S. 202. Go north on 202. As you reach New Hope, go east on PA 179 to the station.

Now and Then: The stretch of track on which the tourist trains travel is strictly a tourist railroad, and a connecting section of track near Ivyland is an active freight line. The road began life as the Northeast Pennsylvania Railroad in 1870 and carried its first passengers to Philadelphia in 1891. It began tourist operations in 1966.

The Station: The New Hope & Ivyland operates out of a restored 1920s station with a ticket booth, a souvenir shop, and a waiting room warmed by a pot-bellied stove.

The Route: The train runs southwest from New Hope to Lahaska. Most of the route is through wooded areas and fields.

Approximate Trip Time: Under one hour

The Ride: Bucks County is a suburban Philadelphia county that has undergone significant changes over the past quarter century, and those changes are visible from the train. Once, the region was primarily rural. Now, it's largely suburban, and along the train's route beautiful old mansions and new suburban homes are visible. So are many wooded areas and some farms.

The ride begins in downtown New Hope and quickly heads out of town, running beside a small scenic stream. The change from rural to suburban has created an attractive habitat for wildlife, and deer and birds are often visible from the train. A conductor provides a thorough history of the line as the train rolls slowly along.

For the shopping enthusiast, the railroad operates Penns Purchase Shuttle Bus. Passengers can leave the train at Lahaska,

New Hope & Ivyland Railroad.

The crew is ready to roll.

board the bus and travel to nearby outlet stores. The bus then brings the passengers back to meet one of the later trains. While the character of the region is changing, the railroad is definitely old-fashioned. A steam locomotive pulls most trains, the passenger cars are from the 1920s, and the station is of the same vintage.

The Region: One of the nice features of this railroad is that it's in the center of a tourist town. Visitors can park their cars and walk all day. The town is full of antique shops, art galleries, restaurants, and bed and breakfast inns, and all are relatively close together. The Delaware River borders the town on the east, and the river provides many recreational opportunities. Close to the railroad is the New Hope Mule Barge which offers a view of life along the canal as it existed in the 1830s. Visitors can take a ride down the canal in a mule-drawn barge with a historian on board.

A few miles down Route 202 from New Hope is Doylestown, another artsy little town. Doylestown was the home of author James Michener, and the Michener Art Museum is here. So is the Mercer Museum which features a collection of American antiques. The entire downtown area features museums, shopping, and dining.

A few miles down the Delaware River from New Hope on PA Route 32 is Washington Crossing Historic Park. It was at this location on Christmas Day in 1776 that Washington's troops staged their historic crossing of the river.

Bucks County still has about a dozen covered bridges, and the closest to New Hope is the Van Sant Bridge which crosses Pidcock Creek about two miles south of town.

Picture Taking: Just down the line from the station is the trestle used for the movie *The Perils of Pauline*. You can easily walk there and see the train as it comes around a curve.

Schedule: The New Hope & Ivyland is one of only two Pennsylvania tourist railroads that operate all year. (Strasburg is the other.)

January through March—Saturday, Sunday: 12 noon, 1, 2, 3 P.M.

The steam locomotive of the New Hope & Ivyland Railroad approaches a trestle.

Late March to mid-April—Weekdays: 12 noon, 1, 2, 3 P.M.; Saturday, Sunday: 11 A.M., 12 noon, 1, 2, 3, 4 P.M.

Mid-April through mid-May—Friday: 12 noon, 1, 2, 3 P.M.; Saturday, Sunday: 11 A.M., 12 noon, 1, 2, 3, 4 P.M.

Week before Memorial Day—Weekdays: 11 A.M., 12 noon, 1, 2, 3 P.M.; Saturday, Sunday: 11 A.M., 12 noon, 1, 2, 3, 4 P.M.

Memorial Day through Labor Day—Daily: 11 A.M., 12 noon, 1, 2, 3, 4 P.M.; Saturday Specials: 5, 7:30 P.M.

September through early November—Weekdays: 12 noon, 1, 2, 3 P.M.; Saturday, Sunday: 11 A.M., 12 noon, 1, 2, 3, 4 P.M.

Remainder of November—Friday: 12 noon, 1, 2, 3 P.M.; Saturday, Sunday: 11 A.M., 12 noon, 1, 2, 3 P.M.

Early December until Sunday before Christmas—Friday, Saturday, Sunday: 10 A.M., 12 noon, 2, 4 P.M.

Week after Christmas—Weekdays: 12 noon, 1, 2, 3 P.M.; Saturday, Sunday: 11 A.M., 12 noon, 1, 2, 3 P.M.

Special Events: Locomotive Cab Rides (you can pay for the thrill of riding in the steam locomotive while it pulls the train) as well as Evening Star Dinner Train; Sunday Brunch Train; Grapevine Express (wine and cheese trains)

Fares:

Adults	$8.50
Seniors (65 and up)	$7.50
Children 2 to 11	$4.50
Children under 2	$1.50

Power: Steam and diesel

Nearby Attractions: New Hope Mule & Barge Company; Washington Crossing Historic Park; Bucks County Playhouse; covered bridges

Tourist Information: Bucks County Tourist Commission, 152 Swamp Rd., Doylestown, PA 18901, telephone 800-836-BUCKS

Nearest Tourist Railroad: Philadelphia Trolleys—38 miles away; East Penn Railroad—53 miles away

Stewartstown—Stewartstown Railroad

Telephone: 717-993-2936

Location and Directions: Stewartstown is in southern York County, about four miles east of Interstate 83 on PA Route 851. The railroad station is in the center of the small town. It's on your left, just after you cross the railroad tracks, as you come in from the west.

Now and Then: The Stewartstown Railroad is strictly a tourist railroad. It began operations in 1885 and operated until 1972 when Hurricane Agnes destroyed much of the line. Tourist operations began in 1985.

The Station: The Stewartstown Railroad operates out of a 1914 station listed on the National Register of Historic Places. The station now has a ticket booth, a souvenir shop, and a waiting room.

The Route: The Stewartstown Railroad runs west through farms and valleys toward New Freedom, where it formerly had an interchange with the Northern Central Railway.

Approximate Trip Time: One and a half hours

Stewartstown Railroad.

Stewartstown Railroad.

The Ride: In its working days, the Stewartstown Railroad had the nickname of "The Farmer's Railroad" because it carried hay, potatoes, wheat, and the products of local canneries to rail connections for shipment to York and Baltimore. In addition, lumber mills, furniture factories and manufacturers used the line. Today, the freight business is gone, but the farms are still around. The line travels through an agricultural area, although much of the ride is actually through wooded areas that border Deer Creek. The train moves slowly, and in many locations it runs along the sides of steep hills where some skilled engineering was necessary to create the right-of-way. The line still uses an 1870 iron bridge that has earned a place on the National Register of Historic Places, as have the 1906 engine house and the depot, as mentioned above (See "The Station").

The ride is comfortable and relaxed. Volunteers operate this line, and they're very friendly and helpful in explaining the history of the line.

The Region: Stewartstown is in southern York County, about 35 miles north of Baltimore (See "The Region" entry for Northern Central Railway in New Freedom).

Picture Taking: Along PA 851 west of Stewartstown

Schedule: The basic schedule is May through early November, with specials on Easter weekend and during the Christmas season.

Mother's Day (early May) through September—Sunday: 1, 3 P.M.

Fall Foliage Trips, October, early November—Saturday, Sunday: 1:30, 3 P.M.

Holidays—Memorial Day, July 4, Labor Day: 1, 3 P.M.

Special Events:

North Pole Express, from weekend after Thanksgiving through weekend before Christmas—Saturday, Sunday: 10 A.M., 12:30, 3 P.M.

Country Breakfast Trains, May through November—third Saturday of each month: 9 A.M.

Fares: Adults are $7.00 and children (3 to 11) are $4.00.
Power: Diesel
Nearby Attractions: Lake Aldred; Harley Davidson Museum in York; Baltimore
Tourist Information: York County Convention and Visitors Bureau, 1 Market Way E., York, PA 17405, telephone 800-673-2429, web site http://yrkpa.kias.com
Nearest Tourist Railroad: Northern Central—eight miles away

Strasburg—Strasburg Railroad

Telephone: 717-687-7522
Location and Directions: Of all of Pennsylvania's tourist railroads, this is the one that benefits most from its location. It's on PA 741, east of Strasburg in eastern Lancaster County, right in the center of Amish Country, a major tourist destination.

Now and Then: The Strasburg is the oldest short-line railroad in the country, and it's the oldest tourist railroad in Pennsylvania. The first train operated in December of 1851, and the first excursion train of the modern era pulled out of the station on January 4, 1959. At the time, expectations were modest. Early revenues were scarcely enough to pay to refill the engine's 50-gallon gasoline tank, but the owners persisted, and by the end of that first season they were sufficiently encouraged to borrow money and begin an expansion project. Today, the Strasburg is easily the busiest tourist railroad in the continental U.S., carrying more than 400,000 passengers a year.

One factor that greatly enhanced the Strasburg's success was the decision to return to steam power. It was Labor Day weekend in 1960 when a steam engine appeared in Strasburg for the first time in 34 years, and revenues soared afterward. Today, the Strasburg has the most extensive operation of all Pennsylvania's tourist railroads.

The Station: The Strasburg has more station offerings than any of Pennsylvania's other tourist railroads, with a rebuilt

Strasburg Railroad.

The nation's oldest short-line railroad rolls through fertile farmlands.

The engineer gives a wave as he prepares to head to Paradise.

Victorian ticket booth, souvenir shops, dining facilities, waiting areas and picnic areas.

The Route: The Strasburg runs four and a half miles from Strasburg to Amtrak's main line in Paradise. For most of its route the train runs through Amish farms.

Approximate Trip Time: Under one hour

The Ride: The ride begins at a restored 1882 Victorian station where passengers obtain tickets and can purchase food and souvenirs. The huge steam engine lurches and moves slowly from the station. On board, passengers can choose from different types of coaches, either carefully restored standard wooden ones or open air observation cars. The deluxe option is a ride in the "Marian," a parlor car with a plush interior and an attendant. The 54-seat "Lee Brenner" is available for lunch on all regularly scheduled hourly trains. The first sight is the Red Caboose Motel, where all the rooms are restored cabooses (see Resting chapter).

The trains move slowly to Paradise, through verdant fields

where Amish farmers work the land with machinery powered by horses and mules. At Groff's Grove, passengers may leave the train and enjoy a picnic, then catch a later train back to Strasburg. At Paradise, the train stops, and the engine does its runaround.

The Region: Strasburg lies in the heart of the nation's most productive non-irrigated agricultural county. Lancaster County produces more than $900 million worth of agricultural commodities annually. Many of the farmers are Amish, and a large tourist industry has grown up around them. The Amish are just a small part of the population of Lancaster County, and the region also has a strong manufacturing past and present. Pennsylvania's only president, James Buchanan, lived in Lancaster.

Lancaster County has an extensive network of rural roads that are excellent for bicycling, and the county ranks second in the country in the number of covered bridges still standing and first in the number still open to cars.

Food is naturally one of the county's main attractions. Pennsylvania Dutch cuisine tends to be substantial, and it's always plentiful. Several local restaurants feature smorgasbords, where diners can eat their fill for one price. In summer, many visitors load up with fresh produce, baked goods, and canned goods at the many roadside stands throughout the area.

Strasburg itself is a small town with a big railroad presence. In addition to the Strasburg Railroad, train attractions include museums, a motel, and shops that sell model trains and train souvenirs.

Picture Taking: Red Caboose Motel, on Esbenshade Road just east of the station

Schedule: The Strasburg Railroad runs almost all year. Only during the first two weeks of January do trains not run. From mid-January until the end of March, trains run only on weekends. From April through November, they run every day. In December trains run on weekends before Christmas, and every day but Thursday during the week between Christmas and New Year's Day.

Mid-January through February—Saturday, Sunday, weather permitting. Call for details.

March—Saturday, Sunday: 12 noon, 1, 2, 3 P.M.

End of March through beginning of May—Monday to Friday: 11 A.M., 12 noon, 1, 2, 3, 4 P.M.; Saturday: 11 A.M., 12 noon, 1, 2, 3, 4, 5, 7* P.M.; Sunday: 12 noon, 1, 2, 3, 4, 5, *7 P.M.

Memorial Day Weekend through end of June—Monday to Friday: 11 A.M., 12 noon, 1, 2, 3 P.M.; Saturday: 11 A.M., 12 noon, 1, 2, 3, 4, 5, 7* P.M.; Sunday: 12 noon, 1, 2, 3, 4, 5, *7 P.M.

End of June through Labor Day—Monday to Saturday: 10, 11, 11:30 A.M., 12 noon, 12:30, 1, 1:30, 2, 2:30, 3, 4, 5, 7* P.M.; Sunday: 12 noon, 12:30, 1, 1:30, 2, 2:30, 3, 4, 5, 7 P.M.

Day after Labor Day through last Sunday in September—Monday to Friday: 11 A.M., 12 noon, 1, 2, 3, 4 P.M.; Saturday: 11 A.M., 12 noon, 1, 2, 3, 4, 6* P.M.; Sunday: 12 noon, 1, 2, 3, 4, 6* P.M.

Last Monday in September through last Sunday in October—Monday to Friday: 11 A.M., 12 noon, 1, 2, 3, 4 P.M.; Saturday: 11 A.M., 12 noon, 1, 2, 3, 4, 6* P.M.; Sunday: 12 noon, 1, 2, 3, 4, 6* P.M.

Halloween Ghost Trains—Saturday before Halloween (or Halloween): 6:30, 7:30, 8:30 P.M. (advance reservations needed)

November—Saturday: 11 A.M., 12 noon, 1, 2, 3 P.M.; Sunday: 12 noon, 1, 2, 3 P.M.

Veterans Day—November 10, 11, 12 noon, 1, 2 P.M.

Friday after Thanksgiving: 12 noon, 1, 2, 3 P.M.

December weekends before Christmas—Saturday: 11 A.M., 12 noon, 1, 2, 3 P.M.; Sunday: 12 noon, 1, 2, 3 P.M.

Week after Christmas—Friday, Saturday, Monday, Tuesday, Wednesday: 11 A.M., 12 noon, 1, 2, 3 P.M.; Sunday: 12 noon, 1, 2, 3 P.M.

* Operation of these trains depends on number of dinner reservations.

Special Events:

Easter Bunny trains (bunny on board)—Easter weekend

Halloween Ghost trains (scary rides in the dark)—Saturday in late October

Santa trains (Santa on all trains)—December weekends before Christmas

Fares: Regular

Adults	$7.75
Children 3 to 11	$4.00

All Day Fare (Unlimited Rides)

Per person	$15.00

Marian Parlor Car

Adults	$12.00
Children 3 to 11	$6.00
Under 3	$2.00

Lee Brenner Dining Car

Adults	$8.75
Children 3 to 11	$5.00
Under 3	$1.00

Group Fares (20 or more)

Adults	$5.75
Children 3 to 11	$3.00

School Fares

Age 3 through Gr. 12	$3.00
Teachers and Adults	$5.75

Power: The Strasburg Railroad uses only steam. The Strasburg's repair shop keeps its locomotives in top condition and also does repair work for other railroads.

Nearby Attractions: The Railroad Museum of Pennsylvania (across the street) (see Museums chapter); the National Toy Train Museum (see Museums chapter); the Choo-Choo Barn (model trains); Central Market in Lancaster; Wheatland (home of President James Buchanan in Lancaster); Sight and Sound Entertainment Centre (Biblical stage productions); American Music Theater; the Strasburg Train Shop. For home-made ice cream, visitors and locals favor the Strasburg Country Store and Creamery at the intersection of PA 741 and PA 896 in downtown Strasburg. An excellent place to stock up on local produce and Amish crafts is a roadside stand on an Amish farm about five miles east of Strasburg on PA 741.

Tourist Information: Pennsylvania Dutch Convention and Visitors Bureau, 501 Greenfield Rd., Lancaster, PA 17601, telephone 800-PA-DUTCH, web site http://www.800padutch.com
   Nearest Tourist Railroad: Brandywine Scenic—36 miles away

Tip: The Strasburg carries more than 400,000 passengers annually, so it's wise to arrive early during busy times, such as summer and Columbus Day weekend.

West Chester—Brandywine Scenic Railroad

Telephone: 610-793-4433
   Location and Directions: This railroad is in a scenic location, but you might miss it if you're not looking for your turn. The closest major road is PA 842, west of West Chester. From 842, turn north on Northbrook Road, which is right beside Northbrook Orchards. The station is straight ahead.
   Now and Then: The Brandywine Scenic is both a tourist and a freight railroad. It runs on the tracks of the Wilmington & Northern Branch of the Reading Company, which originated as the Wilmington & Reading Railroad in 1870.
   The Station: Once a station on the Reading Railroad, Northbrook Station now houses offices, a ticket booth, souvenir shop, waiting room, picnic grove, and snack bar.
   The Route(s): The Brandywine Scenic offers two rides, each of about eight miles. One goes north to Embreeville. The other goes south to Lenape.
   Approximate Trip Time: One and a quarter hours
   The Ride: Brandywine Scenic's line is 16 miles long, and the station lies right in the middle of those 16 miles. Thus, there are two different rides, some going north and some south. In either direction, the scenery is pleasant as the train moves through the rolling hills of Chester County.
   The train takes its name from the river that runs beside the tracks. For much of its route, the line runs beside the Brandywine River. Although Philadelphia isn't far away, the

Brandywine Scenic Railroad. (Courtesy Brandywine Scenic Railroad)

The Brandywine Scenic's locomotive rolls into Northbrook Station.

ride is rural and scenic, and passengers see many sights that aren't visible from a highway. The train rolls through rock cuts and past horse and dairy farms. This is one of the most crooked rail lines anywhere, with many S-curves and only an occasional straight stretch.

Along the line are many remnants of the days when the railroad played a much bigger role in the local economy. Riders can see abandoned sidings, coal tipples, and cattle chutes. The famous King Ranch in Texas has a branch in Chester County, and cattle formerly traveled here by train.

The Region: Chester County has two different personalities. The eastern part of the county is part of the Philadelphia suburbs. The Main Line, an area of stately homes that took its nickname from the Main Line of the Pennsylvania Railroad, is partially in eastern Chester County, but the western part of the county is largely an Amish farming area.

West Chester itself is home to West Chester University. It's a small town with many beautiful old homes. The area surrounding the train station is largely agricultural, and Northbrook Orchards, where visitors can buy fresh produce, is at the intersection of Northbrook Road and PA 842. The Brandywine Valley was home to Andrew Wyeth and his family of painters.

Picture Taking: Route 52 in Lenape or Route 162 in Embreeville

Schedule: The basic schedule is mid-March until Christmas, with trains running Saturday and Sunday at 11 A.M., 12:30, 2, and 3:30 P.M. "Rails to the River" canoe trains operate at 9:30 A.M. on Saturday and Sunday from May through October. One rail car has been converted to carry canoes; canoeists can ride the train upstream and paddle a canoe (available for rental at the station or their own) back down to the station.

Special Events:

Family Fun Weekends (magicians, jugglers, face painters, and singers)—one weekend each month May through September

Good Old Summertime Trains (barbershop music on board and barbecue at the station)—fourth Saturday in June, July, and August

Mother's Day and Father's Day Specials—mothers and fathers ride for half price on their respective days

Fall Foliage Specials—October weekends

Halloween Ghost Trains (children in costume ride for half fare)—weekend closest to Halloween

North Pole Express (Christmas carol singing and Santa on board)—weekends between Thanksgiving and Christmas

Fares: Regular

Adults	$8.00
Seniors (55 and up)	$7.00
Children 2 to 12	$6.00

Special Event

Adults	$10.00
Seniors	$9.00
Children	$8.00

Power: Diesel

Nearby Attractions: Longwood Gardens; Brandywine Battlefield Park; Brandywine River Museum; Phillips Mushroom Museum; Valley Forge

Tourist Information: Chester County Tourist Bureau, 601 Westtown Rd., West Chester, PA 19382-4536, telephone 800-747-0561

Nearest Tourist Railroad: West Chester—six miles away

West Chester—West Chester Railroad Company

Telephone: 610-430-2233

Location and Directions: The station in West Chester is gone, and the railroad operates out of a caboose on Market Street. To reach the station, take U.S. 202 to West Chester. Take the Business District exit and follow Gay Street to the center of town. Then go east on Market Street to the caboose.

Now and Then: Until recently, this stretch of track served as

West Chester Railroad Company. (Courtesy West Chester Railroad Company)

Waiting for movement to the railroad yard. (Courtesy West Chester Railroad Company)

a commuter line for SEPTA, the transportation authority serving the Philadelphia area. The original West Chester Railroad company began operations in 1831 and ran from West Chester to Malvern, where it connected with the Pennsylvania Railroad.

The Station: The line operates between the caboose in West Chester and a nicely maintained station in Glen Mills. In addition, several other old stations are still standing in small towns along the route.

The Route: The line runs from West Chester to Glen Mills, about seven and a half miles.

Approximate Trip Time: One hour. This line has authorization to operate at speeds up to 29 MPH, faster than other tourist railroads.

The Ride: The route follows the Chester Creek through a region that might qualify as a naturalist's delight. Houses are few along the largely wooded route. Deer, foxes, and hawks are often visible from the train.

The Region: Philadelphia is nearby and Chester County has experienced significant suburban development. West Chester is close enough to the big city for residents to commute, but it is by no means a bedroom community. It has its own charm and character and its own university—West Chester U., a state-supported institution.

The surrounding region is home to many large estates and horse farms. Just south of West Chester is the Brandywine Valley, made famous by the Wyeths, the painting family. In the western part of the county are many Amish farms and one of the largest mushroom-growing operations in the world.

Picture Taking: Along PA Route 926 at the station in Westtown. From West Chester, go south on U.S. 202 and east on PA 926.

Schedule: This railroad's scheduled debut is September 1997. No information on train times was available to the author at the time of writing.

Special Events: Special events will be a large part of the operations of the West Chester Railroad Company. Many train runs will tie in with holidays and celebrations.

This caboose trails a center cab and a locomotive. (Courtesy West Chester Railroad Company)

Fares: Adults are $8.00 and children (2 to 12) are $4.00.

Power: Diesel

Nearby Attractions: Longwood Gardens; Franklin Mint Museum; Colonial Pennsylvania Plantation; Brandywine River Museum; Great Valley Nature Center

Tourist Information: Chester County Tourist Bureau, 601 Westtown Rd., West Chester, PA 19382-4536, telephone 800-747-0561

Nearest Tourist Railroad: Brandywine Scenic—six miles away

Northeast Region

Honesdale—Stourbridge Line

Telephone: 717-253-1960 or 800-433-9008

Location and Directions: This one is comparatively easy to find. Honesdale is in the northeastern corner of Pennsylvania, about 30 miles east of Scranton. To get to Honesdale, take U.S. Route 6 from east or west. Route 6 becomes Main Street in Honesdale, and the train station is in the 800 block of Main Street. Purchase tickets at the Wayne County Chamber of Commerce, 742 Main St.

Now and Then: Today, both passengers and freight travel on the Stourbridge Line. On August 9, 1829, the Delaware & Hudson operated the first locomotive on rails in the United States. That train left from the current boarding spot, ran three miles northwest to Seelyville, and returned. The original Stourbridge Lion weighed more than seven tons, instead of the three tons that the builders claimed. It proved too heavy for the rails, and its life on those rails was short but significant.

The Station: Trains board at a municipal parking lot in downtown Honesdale, but it's not really a station.

Approximate Trip Time: One and a half hours for trips to Hawley; trips to Lackawaxen take four and a half hours, including an hour and a half layover in Lackawaxen.

The Route: The train runs beside the Lackawaxen River

79

Stourbridge Line.

from Honesdale to Hawley and Lackawaxen. Hawley is about halfway to Lackawaxen, on the same route.

The Ride: As the train pulls out, passengers can see stonework that was a retaining wall for the Delaware & Hudson Canal. The brick building next to the Chamber of Commerce was the Delaware & Hudson office, and it now houses the Wayne County Historical Society. At the southern end of Honesdale is Moore Business Forms, one of the largest industrial users of the rail service.

Hugging the Lackawaxen River, the Stourbridge Line runs to Lackawaxen, a small town on the Delaware River where Western writer Zane Gray lived. After the first mile, the route is completely rural and very scenic. You'll see several industrial sites in Honesdale and rural beauty over the rest of the route.

The river bends frequently, and so does the train route. Meadows and marshes line the right-of-way, and wildlife is abundant. Shorter rides stop in the small town of Hawley, and some include a stopover for sightseeing and dining.

On many of the rides the sponsors provide entertainment tied to a theme, such as Halloween or Christmas.

The Region: Honesdale is on the northern edge of the Pocono Mountains, a region filled with recreational opportunities, such as golf courses, resorts, and ski slopes. Local radio stations refer to the area as "The Lake Region," and a look at a map shows many lakes and ponds throughout the area. The largest is Lake Wallenpaupack, which is a major vacation destination. Boaters and swimmers enjoy its waters, and vacation homes ring its shores.

Honesdale is a pleasant small town with a busy Main Street that's still the primary shopping district. Tourism is a major industry in the area, and Honesdale is home to certain types of businesses that other towns of 5,000 might not have, such as a health food store and a gourmet coffee restaurant. Signs tell drivers to stop to let pedestrians cross the street, and drivers heed the signs. The town itself is a small flat area surrounded by hills that rise steeply on all sides.

A visit to the Wayne County Museum will give you a good look at the railroad history of the region. A "gravity railroad" once hauled coal from Scranton and Carbondale to Honesdale, where it went onto barges for shipment to New York and Philadelphia. At the museum, you can sit in an old railroad car and watch a movie about the region's railroads. Beside the "movie theater" is a full-sized reproduction of the original Stourbridge Lion.

One of the region's big events is the Wayne County Fair, which takes place every August at the Wayne County Fairgrounds, just north of Honesdale on PA 191.

Picture Taking: In Honesdale, about a quarter mile south of the station is a pedestrian overpass.

Schedule: The best piece of advice is to call ahead. In 1996, the Stourbridge Line operated on some but not all Saturdays and Sundays from late March until December. Most of the rides operate in conjunction with a specific holiday or theme.

Special Events:
Bunny Runs—the two Saturdays before Easter

Great Train Robbery Runs—Sundays in July and August
Dinner Theater—middle Saturday of August
Bavarian Festival—fourth Saturday of August
Fall Foliage—first three Saturdays and first two Sundays in October
Halloween Fun—Saturday before Halloween
Santa Express—first weekend and following Saturday in December

Fares: Fares vary according to the event. They range from $10 for regular rides to $40 for the Dinner Theater Train in August.

Power: Diesel

Nearby Attractions: Lake Region; Pocono Mountains

Tourist Information: Wayne County Chamber of Commerce, 742 Main St., Honesdale, PA 18431, telephone 800-433-9008

Nearest Tourist Railroad: Steamtown—30 miles away

Jim Thorpe—Rail Tours, Inc.

Telephone: 717-325-4606

Location and Directions: Jim Thorpe is in east-central Pennsylvania, along the Lehigh River. U.S. Route 209 is the main road into town. From the Northeast Extension of the Pennsylvania Turnpike, exit at Lehighton and go south on 209. The station is at the center of town.

Now and Then: Rail Tours, Inc. carries only passengers on a route that was originally part of the Nesquehoning Valley Railroad, which opened in 1870. Before then, the Mauch Chunk Switchback Railroad used gravity to carry coal down the mountain to the Lehigh Canal. Mules then pulled the cars back uphill to the mines. By 1872, the railroads served the mines directly, and the Switchback Railroad lost its original use. It then became a tourist railroad, functioning as the world's longest roller coaster. The Switchback Railroad is completely gone, but its right-of-way is still intact. It now serves as a hiking trail, and a local group is hoping to reconstruct the Switchback Railroad as a tourist attraction.

Rail Tours, Inc.

A D & H caboose sits in the yard in downtown Jim Thorpe.

The Station: A restored Central of New Jersey station houses a ticket booth, a waiting room, and offices.

The Route: This is a water route, running beside a river, a creek, and a lake. The ride begins beside the Lehigh River, turns west beside the Nesquehoning Creek, and eventually comes to Lake Hauto on the longer routes. The route initially parallels U.S. Route 209. After it passes through the town of Nesquehoning, it runs close to PA Route 54.

Approximate Trip Time: 40 minutes, one and three-quarter hours, two and a half hours, or two and three-quarter hours, depending on the length of the ride chosen

The Ride: Called *Yesterday's Train Today*, it begins at a beautifully maintained Central Railroad of New Jersey depot in the center of downtown Jim Thorpe. It starts out going north along the Lehigh River, then turns west beside the Nesquehoning Creek. The basic ride travels from Jim Thorpe to Milepost 5 and returns. Longer rides go farther on the same line, to Lake Hauto (20-mile round trip) and Hometown (32-mile round trip). The Flaming Foliage Ramble rolls through miles of woodland, along Nesquehoning Creek, past Lake Hauto and through Hometown on its way to Haucks. It's also the same route as the other rides, but even a bit longer. Like many other Pennsylvania railroads, this one runs beside a creek for most of its length. Mountains rise steeply around the line, and in autumn the fall foliage is spectacular. The area is heavily wooded, and it's quite common to see wildlife, such as deer, along the route.

Although it runs beside water, this line wasn't easy to build. In many places, workers had to blast and cut the line from the side of a mountain. Beside the line, the mountain rises so steeply that climbing it would be a challenge. Rhododendrons and ferns grow profusely, and reminders of the region's coal-mining past are numerous.

The Region: Coal is the reason for Jim Thorpe's existence. Originally named Mauch Chunk, Jim Thorpe is in Carbon County, a major source of anthracite coal. Compared to more plentiful bituminous coal, anthracite is harder and burns more cleanly.

In 1954, Mauch Chunk changed its name to Jim Thorpe to honor the famous athlete. Thorpe had no ties to Mauch Chunk during his life, but he wound up here when the town leaders offered his widow a final resting place for her husband.

Jim Thorpe has undergone a metamorphosis from a coal town to a tourist town. On warm days, visitors fill the town to enjoy train rides, recreation and shopping. Carbon County is a rugged land that's home to several state parks and many lakes.

Picture Taking: Bridge on Route 93 in Nesquehoning or at the station in Jim Thorpe

Schedule: The basic operating schedule is weekends and holidays from May through October.

Yesterday's Train Today (10-mile round trip to Milepost 5)— Saturday, Sunday and holidays from Mother's Day Weekend through Labor Day: 12 noon, 1, 2 P.M.; September weekends: 12 noon, 1, 2, 3 P.M.

Hometown Trestle Specials (32-mile round trip)—Saturdays from end of May through end of August—3 P.M.

Lake Hauto Specials (20-mile round trip)—Sundays and holidays from Memorial Day Weekend through Labor Day Weekend: 3 P.M.

Flaming Foliage Rambles (34-mile round trip to Haucks)— Weekends in October except final two Sundays and last Saturday: 10 A.M., 2:15 P.M.; final two Sundays and last Saturday: 1:15 P.M.

Special Events: Additional trains are put on at Easter and Christmas.

Fares: Yesterday's Train Today
                 (basic ride)

Adults	$5.00
Children 2 to 11	$3.00

                 Lake Hauto Specials

Adults	$8.00
Children 2 to 11	$4.00

Hometown Trestle Specials
Adults	$9.00
Children 2 to 11	$5.00

Flaming Foliage Rambles
Adults	$14.00
Children 2 to 11	$7.00

Santa Claus Rides (40 minutes)
Adults	$7.00
Children 9 to 11	$4.00

Note: Limit of two free child tickets with paying adult

Power: Steam and diesel

Nearby Attractions: Shops in Jim Thorpe; Packer Mansion; Lehigh River; Mauch Chunk Lake; Pocono Mountains; Lehigh Gorge State Park

Tourist Information: Carbon County Tourist Promotion Agency, P.O. Box 90, Jim Thorpe, PA 18229, telephone 717-325-3673

Nearest Tourist Railroad: Wanamaker, Kempton & Southern —42 miles away

Lewisburg—West Shore Rail Excursions, Lewisburg & Buffalo Creek Railroad and West Shore Railroad

Telephone: 717-524-4337

Location and Directions: Easy to find, the station is on U.S. Route 15, just north of Lewisburg, and about 5 miles south of Interstate 80.

Now and Then: These two lines carry tourists only on tracks formerly owned by the Reading Railroad.

The Station: Delta Place Station is a former Reading Railroad station that houses a ticket booth, a souvenir shop, and a waiting room.

The Route: The Lewisburg & Buffalo Creek Railroad runs along the Susquehanna River to Winfield. The West Shore

West Shore Rail Excursions.

Railroad takes a different route, running west to Mifflinburg, parallel to Route 45.

Approximate Trip Time: The West Shore Railroad, which runs only on Sunday, makes a round trip to Mifflinburg in approximately two hours. All other trips run on the Lewisburg & Buffalo Creek Railroad and take one and a quarter hours.

The Ride: Lewisburg is a college town, and the Lewisburg & Buffalo Creek ride passes through downtown and the campus of Bucknell University before it hugs the west branch of the Susquehanna River for the remainder of its journey to Winfield. For much of the ride, only the river and the trees are visible. The cliffs of the Buffalo Mountains loom above, and the ride is very leisurely and tranquil.

The Susquehanna River begins life in Cooperstown, New York, and it's quite scenic as it cuts through the center of Pennsylvania. In most places, the river is so shallow and rocky that it's never supported transportation. It is, however, quite popular with recreational boaters, and on summer days they're all over the water.

Souvenirs and snacks are available in the mail car.

This station is the boarding place for both lines.

On Sunday 2 P.M. rides during the summer (the West Shore Railroad), the train takes a different route, going west through a beautiful agricultural valley to the small town of Mifflinburg. The Sunday route parallels PA Route 45 as it passes through Amish and Mennonite farms. The Buffalo Valley is scenic and green, and Mifflinburg is a small town with a Victorian flavor.

The Region: This is an area of contrasts. To the west of Lewisburg are fertile farmlands. To the southeast are coal fields. In the area right around Lewisburg, the farms end where the mountains begin.

Lewisburg features both Victorian and Federal architecture. Distinctive lampposts light much of the town, and the downtown shopping area is quite pleasant. Bucknell University covers 300 acres and offers a broad selection of cultural and athletic events.

Picture Taking: West Shore Railroad—many points along Route 45. The line is parallel to and just north of the highway. Buffalo Creek Railroad—Huffnagel Park in downtown Lewisburg

Schedule: The line's basic schedule is from the beginning of April through the end of October, with additional Christmas runs. All rides are on the Lewisburg & Buffalo Creek line, except for Sunday 2 P.M. rides, which are West Shore Railroad rides.

Easter weekend through May—Saturday, Sunday: 2 P.M.

End of May through August—Saturday: 11:30 A.M., 2 P.M.

June through August—Sunday: 11:30 A.M., 2 P.M.

Mid-June until Labor Day Weekend—Tuesday through Sunday: 11:30 A.M., 2 P.M.

Special Events:

Dinner trains—first Saturday of the month, May through October: 6 P.M.

Easter Bunny Express—Saturday before Easter: 11 A.M., 12:30, 2 P.M.

Wake Up the Bears—First Saturday, Sunday of April: 2 P.M.

Cartoon Express—Third Saturday, Sunday of April: 2 P.M.

School Field Trips—Tuesday through Friday, May, first week of June: 10 A.M., 12 noon

Mother's Day Dinner Train: 11:30 A.M., 2 P.M.

Father's Day Dinner Train: 11:30 A.M., 2 P.M.

Fall Foliage Tours—October weekends

Haunted Train Rides—Friday through Monday before Halloween: 6:30, 8 P.M.

Santa Rides—First weekend in December: 11 A.M., 12:30, 2 P.M.

Fares: Lewisburg & Buffalo Creek

Adults	$7.00
Seniors (60 and up)	$6.50
Children 3 to 11	$4.00

West Shore

Adults	$9.00
Seniors (60 and up)	$8.50
Children 3 to 11	$5.00

Power: Diesel

Nearby Attractions: Walnut Acres, the nation's first organic farm; Bucknell University; Mifflinburg Buggy Museum; the Motorcar and Hand Railcar Show on the middle weekend of August; the Buffalo Valley Antique Machinery Show on the second weekend in October

Tourist Information: Susquehanna Valley Visitors Bureau, 219D Hafer Rd., Lewisburg, PA 17837, telephone 717-524-7234

Nearest Tourist Railroad: Middletown & Hummelstown—72 miles away; Tioga Central—77 miles away; Pioneer Tunnel Coal Mine—40 miles away

Scranton—Steamtown National Historic Site

Telephone: 717-346-0660

Location and Directions: Take Interstate 81 to Scranton. Take exit 53, the Central Scranton Expressway, and go west to the third traffic light. Turn left and go one and a half blocks.

Steamtown National Historic Site excursions.

Pass the Steamtown Mall and turn left on Lackawanna Avenue.

Now and Then: Steamtown carries only passengers on former Delaware, Lackawanna & Western tracks. Scranton was once a major rail hub, with action centered at the Lackawanna Station, which is now the Lackawanna Station Hotel.

The Station: The site has a ticket booth and a souvenir shop, in addition to all the other buildings that go with the multi-million-dollar federal museum at the Steamtown National Historic Site (see Museums chapter).

The Route: The line goes uphill to Moscow through a heavily wooded area.

Approximate Trip Time: Two and a half hours

The Ride: Rolling through the mountains, the line rises and rises as it climbs out of Scranton. All the way to Moscow, the train seems to be going uphill. Through most of its route, the line travels through woods and beside a creek. Compared to other tourist lines, this one seems to be zooming along, although its speed is still far below that of a bullet train. The conductors are one of the highlights of the ride. They talk to the passengers, especially children, and answer any and all railroading questions.

In Moscow, the train stops for the engine to move from one end of the train to the other, and this provides excellent photo opportunities. Some of the workers on the trains are National Park rangers, and they have a thorough knowledge of the trains. Food and souvenirs are available at the turnaround area, and there's a little picnic area.

The line passes the Scranton Reservoir, and on the way back to Scranton, the train and the water move downhill together. Building this line was a challenge, as the many cuts through rock show, and the train has a much easier run on the return to Scranton.

The museum is open all year.

The Region: Scranton is the largest city in an area of northeastern Pennsylvania commonly known as "The Coal Regions." The coal mined in the region is anthracite, or hard, coal. It burns more cleanly than soft, or bituminous, coal. Some coal mining continues today, but the industry has actually been in decline since its peak year of 1917. Coal built Scranton, and industrialists built railroads to carry coal from Scranton to markets around the East. Coal and iron shaped Scranton's economic destiny.

Surrounding Scranton is the Pocono Mountain region, a large area of northeastern Pennsylvania filled with rugged hills, golf courses, beautiful waterfalls, and recreational opportunities.

Picture Taking: Overpass in the yard at Steamtown

Schedule: The basic schedule is Fridays, Saturdays, and Sundays from Memorial Day through early November.

Memorial Day Weekend—Friday: 1 P.M.; Saturday, Sunday, Monday: 12 noon, 3 P.M.

Last Weekend in May through June—Friday, Saturday, Sunday: 1 P.M.

July 4 through Labor Day weekend—Friday, Saturday, Sunday, holidays: 12 noon, 3 P.M.

September weekends after Labor Day—Saturday, Sunday: 12 noon, 3 P.M.

October through first weekend in November—Friday, Saturday, Sunday, holiday: 12 noon, 3 P.M.

Special Events:
National Park Week—Third week of April
Armed Forces Day—Third Saturday in May
Steamtown Rail Expo—Labor Day weekend
Toys For Tots Train—First weekend in December

Fares:

Adults	$10.00
Seniors (62 and up)	$8.00
Children under 16	$5.00
Motorcoach Tour Groups	$400.00

Power: Steam

Nearby Attractions: Steamtown National Historic Site Museum (see Museums chapter); Pennsylvania Anthracite Heritage Museum; Scranton Iron Furnaces; Pocono Downs Race Track (harness racing); Pocono Raceway (auto racing); Lackawanna County Stadium (AAA baseball); Pocono Mountains

Tourist Information: Pennsylvania's Northeast Territory Visitors Bureau, 201 Hangar Rd., Suite 203, Avoca, PA 18641, telephone 800-22-WELCOME, web site http://www.travelfile.com

Nearest Tourist Railroad: Stourbridge—30 miles away

Wellsboro—Tioga Central Railroad

Telephone: 717-724-0990

Location and Directions: The Tioga Central is in Wellsboro Junction, on PA Route 287, just north of U.S. Route 6, about 3 miles west of Wellsboro. Wellsboro is in north-central Pennsylvania, about 15 miles south of the New York border.

Now and Then: During the week, the Wellsboro and Corning Railroad hauls freight on the line. On weekends, tourists take over. Tourist operations begin outside Wellsboro, but

Tioga Central Railroad.

freight traffic goes right into town. The line is largely original grade (right-of-way) of the Tioga Railroad, which opened in 1840. Later, it became part of the New York Central's Pennsylvania Division. In its previous life, it traveled through Pennsylvania's Grand Canyon to Jersey Shore. There, it connected with major lines that ran along the Susquehanna River.

The Station: For the Tioga Central, the station is a railroad car in a parking lot. Tickets and souvenirs are available.

The Route: The train runs north along Route 287 to Hammond Lake.

Approximate Trip Time: One and a half hours; two and a half hours for the dinner trains

The Ride: The Tioga Central carries passengers along Crooked Creek and north to Hammond Lake. One of its most popular runs is the dinner train, which operates on Saturday nights and is often sold out weeks or months in advance.

Like many rail lines in Pennsylvania, this stretch of track hugs a creek while hills rise steeply all around it. The line runs parallel to PA 287 for most of its route and passes through several tiny towns. The scenery is spectacular, and an open car provides an excellent viewing site. In this lightly populated area, wildlife is abundant. Passengers frequently spot ospreys, blue herons, deer, and occasionally may even eye a bear.

The Tioga Central is a railroad with an interesting history. Through 1994, it operated in New York state. At that time, Wellsboro was upgrading its rail line to retain its major industries, which depend heavily on rail service. When the Tioga Central lost its lease in New York, it was able to find a new home in Pennsylvania.

The Region: The area around Wellsboro is one of Pennsylvania's favorite vacation areas. The primary attraction is Pennsylvania's Grand Canyon, and the biggest town nearby is Wellsboro, a picturesque place in Pennsylvania's northern mountains. Modeled after English towns, it has a town green, a beautiful old hotel, and old-fashioned gas lights. No suburban malls have come to Wellsboro, and downtown is still the main shopping district.

Pennsylvania's Grand Canyon is less famous than the one in Arizona, but it's still a great attraction. Pine Creek runs through the canyon, and the rims of the canyon walls are about 1,000 feet above the water. Canoeists, hikers, and bicyclists enjoy active recreation in the region. Bicyclists can now ride on a rail trail through the canyon, a trail where trains used to run.

Picture Taking: Many places along Route 287

Schedule: The basic schedule is weekends from early May through October.

Second weekend in May through third weekend in October—Saturday, Sunday: 11 A.M., 1, 3 P.M.

In addition, Fall Foliage Trains operate on the second and third Thursdays and the third Wednesday of October, a Thanksgiving train operates on Thanksgiving Day, and a Christmas train operates on the first Saturday of December.

Special Events:

Saturday evening dinner trains, 40-mile (extra-long) round trip—June through October: 5:30 p.m.

Wellsboro Rail Days—final weekend in October: Saturday 9, 11 A.M., 1, 6 P.M.; Sunday 8:30 A.M., 3 P.M.

Fares:

Adults	$10.00
Seniors (60 and up)	$9.00
Children 6 to 12	$5.00
Dinner Trains	$28.00

Power: Diesel

Nearby Attractions: Pennsylvania Grand Canyon; town of Wellsboro; Hammond Lake; County Fair; Rail Days, which are a celebration of the region's rail history, with model trains, a swap meet, and presentations by local historians

Tourist Information: Tioga County Tourist Promotion Agency, 114 Main St., Wellsboro, PA 16901, telephone 800-332-6718

Nearest Tourist Railroad: West Shore—77 miles away

Southwest Region

Altoona and Johnstown—Amtrak (Horseshoe Curve)

Horseshoe Curve, Altoona 814-946-0834
Amtrak Altoona 1231 11th Ave. 814-946-1100
Amtrak Johnstown 47 Walnut St. 814-535-3313

Location and Directions: To Horseshoe Curve, which is five miles west of Altoona: Take the Pennsylvania Turnpike to exit 11 and go north on U.S. 220. At Third Avenue, go west to PA 764. At Burgoon Street, go west across the railroad tracks. Make the first left, onto Beale Street. Then go right on 40th Street, which will take you to the Curve.

To Altoona Station: Take the Pennsylvania Turnpike to exit 11 and go north on U.S. 220. Take U.S. 220 to 17th Street. Go west into the city, across the tracks to 11th Avenue and turn right.

To Johnstown Station: Take the Pennsylvania Turnpike to exit 10. Go north on U.S. 219 to PA 56. Go north on PA 56 into Johnstown. The station is at the north end of the city, within walking distance of the Incline and the Flood Museum.

Now and Then: The Curve is still in heavy daily use as a major freight route, and two Amtrak trains pass in each direction every day. For train watchers, the Curve is a superb location. Trains struggle up and thunder down the mountain all day and all night.

When the Curve opened, Pittsburgh was still a western frontier.

Horseshoe Curve: two Conrail diesels push a long coal train through the Curve. A mile ahead, three more diesels will pull the train.

Located between Altoona and Johnstown, this amazing engineering feat conquered the Allegheny Mountains, which are in essence the Eastern Continental Divide. The Alleghenies aren't high, as mountains go, but they are steep, and were a major obstacle to westward expansion.

The Horseshoe Curve made that expansion possible. Before the railroad, a trip across Pennsylvania took about 20 days on a slow freight wagon. Travelers from Philadelphia to Pittsburgh faced 300 miles of bad road, steep mountains, numerous small streams, and the mile-wide Susquehanna River. West of Pittsburgh, the terrain becomes much more forgiving and stays that way all the way to the Rockies.

Opening in 1854, the Horseshoe Curve immediately became a major tourist attraction, and it's still going strong today. Dozens of freight trains on a major Conrail route use the Curve every day, and a handful of Amtrak trains round the Curve daily.

Crews perform maintenance on one track while Conrail thunders over another.

The funicular railroad carries passengers to track level.

No tourist railroad uses the Curve, but the National Park Service conducts a program called "Tracks Through Time" that serves the same purpose. From early June through the middle of October, National Park Service rangers provide a narrative tour of the Curve on Amtrak's *Pennsylvanian* between Altoona and Johnstown.

The Station: The Altoona Station is part of a modern complex that includes a bus station. The Johnstown Station is a handsome, older building whose capacity exceeds its current traffic.

The Route: Johnstown and Altoona are on opposite sides of a mountain. From Johnstown, the tracks follow the South Fork of the Conemaugh River to the highest point on the line, the twin tunnels in Gallitzin. From Gallitzin, it's downhill to the Curve and Altoona.

Approximate Trip Time: One hour in each direction

The Ride: Horseshoe Curve differs from the other tourist railroad attractions in Pennsylvania. To ride through Horseshoe Curve, you must board an Amtrak train in either Johnstown or Altoona. Because Amtrak runs only two trains a day in each direction, you must time your ride properly or you won't be able to get back to your departure point on the same day. Amtrak's schedules change frequently, so you'll have to check before you ride.

In the summer of 1997, the best way to do the ride was to board a 9:48 A.M. train in Johnstown. That train arrived in Altoona at 10:50, and the next westbound to Johnstown left at 2:01 P.M.

On Thursdays, Fridays, and Saturdays from June through October, the National Park Service operated narrated excursions that left Johnstown on the 9:48 A.M. train and returned on the 2:01. During the layover, visitors could tour the Railroaders Memorial Museum (see Museums chapter), which is adjacent to the station in Altoona.

Leaving from either Johnstown or Altoona, the train climbs for the first half of the ride and descends for the second half.

Leaving from Altoona, passengers peer eagerly out the window as the train heads west. At the highest point on the route is Gallitzin, where the train plunges into darkness as it passes through the long Gallitzin Tunnels. Just west of Gallitzin, the tracks enter the Conemaugh River Valley and follow the river into Johnstown, passing through several small towns along the way. All the while, freight trains share the route.

The Region: As famous as the Curve may be, it's not the only famous feature of the region. The Johnstown Flood of 1889 also has a place in history. As you ride the train, it's easy to see how Johnstown could be the victim of a flood. From South Fork, the site of the dam that broke, it's all downhill to Johnstown. On May 31, 1889, a neglected dam at a club for the wealthy gave way. A wall of water roared down the narrow valley, 2,209 people died, and a city that was vibrant and prosperous in the morning was nothing but muddy ruins in the afternoon.

Johnstown recovered from the flood and once again became a prosperous steel and coal center, but the flood has always been a major part of its identity. Shortly after the flood, the town constructed the Johnstown Incline to carry people from downtown to the new suburb of Westmont, which sits on top of a big hill, hundreds of feet above the original city (see Inclines chapter). After the flood, many people with money moved up to Westmont, while the working class remained down in the city and in the path of future floods. Nothing on the scale of the flood of 1889 has happened since, but in 1936 and 1977 floods triggered by thunderstorms damaged the area severely.

Manufacturing and mining define this region. With its steep mountains, it's not friendly to agriculture. Johnstown was a major steel city, and Altoona was a railroad city. Steep mountains dominate the entire region, and forests still cover most of the land.

Picture Taking: The visitor center at the Curve

Schedule: Amtrak operates two trains daily in each direction. The following are the summer 1997 times and are subject to change.

Leave Johnstown at 9:48 A.M. (narrated); arrive in Altoona at 10:50 A.M.

Leave Altoona at 2:01 P.M. (narrated); arrive in Johnstown at 2:59 P.M.

Leave Johnstown at 2:30 P.M.; arrive in Altoona at 3:30 P.M.

Leave Altoona at 7:53 P.M.; arrive in Johnstown at 8:57 P.M.

Special Events: Trips narrated by National Park Service officers from early June through October

Fares: Regular rides are $13.00 and narrated trips (in separate cars on regular trains) are $20.00.

Power: Diesel

Nearby Attractions: The Altoona Railroaders Museum beside the Amtrak station in Altoona (see Museums chapter); the Johnstown Incline (see Inclines chapter); the Allegheny Portage Railroad Museum (see Museums chapter); the Gallitzin Tunnels and the small observation area on top of the tunnels in downtown Gallitzin; the Seldom Seen Mine (see Mines chapter); Horseshoe Curve Visitors Center

Tourist Information: Allegheny Mountain Convention and Visitors Bureau, Logan Valley Mall, Route 220 & Goods Lane, Altoona, PA 16602, telephone 800-84-ALTOONA

Nearest Tourist Railroad: Bellefonte Historical—43 miles away (from Altoona)

Orbisonia—East Broad Top Railroad

Telephone: 814-447-3011

Location and Directions: Orbisonia is in south-central Pennsylvania, about 110 miles southeast of Pittsburgh. From east or west, take the Pennsylvania Turnpike to exit 13, Fort Littleton, U.S. 522. Orbisonia is 19 miles north of the exit on 522.

Now and Then: The East Broad Top now carries only pleasure passengers, although some people involved with the railroad have hopes of restoring freight service. The line began in

East Broad Top Railroad. (Photo by Ron Morgan)

The EBT steams through rural Huntington County. (Photo by Ron Morgan)

The steps are down and the East Broad Top is ready for passengers to come aboard.

The narrow-gauge EBT has been using the same passenger cars since the 1880s.

1874 to haul coal, and it ceased freight operations in 1956. Tourist excursions began in 1960.

The Station: Orbisonia Station is a delightfully maintained old railroad station with ticket booths, souvenir shops, and offices.

The Route: The tracks run through the picturesque Aughwick Valley, past burger and fries restaurants, through back yards, farms and fields. For much of the route, the tracks lie close to U.S. 522. Mountains rise steeply on the east and west, and in many places passengers can reach out and touch the overhanging trees.

Approximate Trip Time: One and a half hours

The Ride: *Authentic* may be the best word to describe the East Broad Top Railroad. Originally chartered as the East Broad Top Railroad and Coal Company, the EBT's primary function was to move the bituminous coal mined in Huntingdon County, coal that still powers the trains. The line also carried passengers on the 33-mile route between Mount Union and Woodvale.

What makes a ride on the EBT so realistic is that the equipment is the railroad's original rolling stock. The passenger cars have been working on the EBT since 1882, and they were already used when they came to Huntingdon County, having served on the Boston, Revere Beach and Lynn line in Massachusetts. The steam locomotives arrived between 1911 and 1918. This railroad has been designated an Endangered National Historic Landmark.

A ride on the EBT is truly a sensual experience. First, you'll see the black smoke and the white steam rising from the engine. Then you'll hear the locomotive's ear-piercing whistle, and finally you'll smell the smoke as the train heads out of the station.

The ride definitely isn't a smooth one, and that's part of the charm on a narrow-gauge line. While standard railroad gauge is 4 feet, 8½ inches, the rails on the EBT are only 36 inches apart. As a result, when the train rounds a bend, it leans significantly.

The ride begins in Orbisonia and travels about five miles north to a picnic area called Colgate Grove. If you ride on one of the first two trains of the day, you can take a lunch along and return on a later train.

The EBT operates only during warm weather months, and one of the highlights is definitely the open car. Passengers sitting here get the full effect of the steam engine, including the cinders that fly out of the engine and land everywhere. With its wooden benches, the open car isn't the most comfortable railroad car in the world, but it's one of the most popular.

The Region: Rockhill Furnace/Orbisonia Station has a population of only 400, and the railroad is the major attraction. Huntingdon County has a population of about 45,000, and forests and mountains cover much of the region.

The biggest attraction for visitors is Raystown Lake, an artificial lake on the Juniata River. Surrounding it are many types of recreational activities, ranging from camping to tour boats to Go-Karts to parasail rides.

Huntingdon is the largest town in the county. It's the county seat and home to Juniata College. The main line of Amtrak and Conrail passes through Huntingdon and Mount Union, and the EBT formerly interchanged with the Pennsylvania Railroad at Mount Union.

Picture Taking: All along Route 522

Schedule: From the beginning of June through late October, Saturdays and Sundays at 11 A.M., 1, 3 P.M.

Special Events: None

Fares: $9.00; luxury cars (which have stained glass windows and softer seats) $10.00

Power: Steam

Nearby Attractions: Raystown Lake

Tourist Information: Raystown Country Visitors Bureau, 241 Mifflin St., Huntingdon, PA 16652, telephone 800-269-4696, web site http://www.raystown.org

Nearest Tourist Railroad: Bellefonte Historical—66 miles away

Scottdale—Laurel Highlands Railroad

Telephone: 412-887-4568

Location and Directions: The boarding area is in downtown Scottdale, on South Broadway, beside a Sheetz convenience store. (In the summer of 1997, local residents began a drive to raise funds to construct a new station, but at the time of writing there was no station yet.) Scottdale is in southwestern Pennsylvania, just west of U.S. 119, on PA 819. Take the Pennsylvania Turnpike (PA 76) or Interstate 70 to New Stanton and go south on U.S. 119.

Now and Then: The Laurel Highlands Railroad, also known as the Highlander, operates only as a tourist line. It runs on sections of track formerly owned by the Pennsylvania Railroad and the Baltimore & Ohio. The B & O tracks date back to 1871 and the Pennsylvania ones to 1873.

The Station: The main boarding area in Scottdale isn't really a station. It's a parking lot.

The Route: The Highlander runs from Scottdale to Youngwood, paralleling U.S. Route 119. On the way, the train stops at Mount Pleasant, and one can take a shortened version of the ride by boarding there.

Approximate Trip Time: One hour or two and a half hours

The Ride: The Highlander travels through a scenic valley in the Laurel Highlands of southwestern Pennsylvania. This is a region of small towns and farms, and the biggest economic force was the mining of coal and coke. The railroad's initial purpose was to transport those commodities. Today, the Highlander runs through an area called the Connellsville Coal and Coke Field.

The ride is leisurely. The little steam engine works hard to conquer several steep grades. Along the route, many industrial sites are visible. Some are still working, and some are abandoned. The train rolls along past houses, farms and fields, and it stops and turns around in Youngwood. There you can visit a very nice railroad museum, located in the former railroad

Laurel Highlands Railroad. (Courtesy Laurel Highlands Railroad)

The Laurel Highlands runs on former Pennsylvania Railroad and Baltimore & Ohio rights-of-way.

depot, which details the history of the railroad in the region.
The Region: Scottdale owes its name to the railroad. Thomas
Alexander Scott was president of the Pennsylvania Railroad in
the 1870s, and the town changed its name to honor him when
his company built a line into the area.

The Laurel Highlands was once the retreat of wealthy Pittsburgh industrialists. Today, the region is popular with vaca-
tioners of more modest means, especially outdoor enthusiasts.
White-water rafters enjoy the Youghiogheny (Yuck' uh gay nee)
River, and the town of Ohiopyle is a favorite place to begin a
rafting expedition. One of America's most famous homes,
Fallingwater, built by Frank Lloyd Wright, is in Mill Run.

In spring and autumn, the region is bright and beautiful.
Wildflowers and mountain laurel bloom in spring, and the
forests burst into brilliant reds, yellows, and golds in autumn.
Mount Davis, Pennsylvania's highest point at 3,213 feet, is in
Somerset County, southeast of Scottdale.

Picture Taking: Youngwood Station, Mount Pleasant Station

Schedule: The basic schedule is Saturdays and Sundays from
May through October. The rides originate in Scottdale, and on
Sundays you can also board at the east end of Mount Pleasant
at Cook's Hobby and Train Shop on PA Route 31, approxi-
mately three-quarters of an hour after the train leaves
Scottdale.

Saturday: 11 A.M., 12:15, 3:30 P.M.

Sunday: 11 A.M., 1:15, 3:30 P.M.

Special Events:

Great Train Robbery (the Over the Hill Gang, riders on
horses, will "rob" the passengers)—early August

Civil War Reenactment (a re-creation of a skirmish involving
one of General Lee's scouting parties that allegedly came into
this region and stole a train)—Labor Day Weekend

Fall Foliage Rides—October.

Fares:	One-hour trips	
Adults		$7.00
Children 5 to 12		$5.00

Two-and-a-half-hour trips
Adults $12.00
Children 5 to 12 $9.00
Power: Steam
Nearby Attractions: Youghiogheny River Trail (rail trail); Fallingwater (Frank Lloyd Wright's masterpiece); Ohiopyle State Park
Tourist Information: Laurel Highlands Visitors Bureau, 120 E. Main St., Ligonier, PA 15658, telephone 800-925-7669
Nearest Tourist Railroad: Pennsylvania Trolley Museum—49 miles away

Northwest Region

Bellefonte—Bellefonte Historical Railroad

Telephone: 814-355-0311

Location and Directions: Bellefonte is in Centre County, just south of Interstate 80 on PA 150 or PA 26. State College is about 12 miles south on PA 150. The station in Bellefonte is right in the center of town, at High and Water, beside Talleyrand Park.

Now and Then: The Bellefonte Historical Railroad is strictly a tourist operation, but the Nittany & Bald Eagle freight trains use the rails during the week. Rail operations began here in 1859 when Bellefonte & Snow Shoe Railroad was built to transport coal from rich deposits in the region.

The Station: A nicely-restored Pennsylvania Railroad station houses the ticket office and a small museum of Centre County railroading.

The Route: The Bellefonte Historical has access to more than 60 miles of track in Centre, Blair and Clinton counties, and operates several different routes.

Approximate Trip Time: One and a half hours

The Ride: All of the lines run beside creek beds for much of their routes as they meander through the mountains and between small towns.

One route stops at Curtin Village, a restored iron-making

Bellefonte Historical Railroad.

The Bellefonte Historical Railroad operates from a restored station in a Victorian town.

"plantation" (or forge) with an ironmaster's mansion. Another route travels to Sayers Dam. There, passengers can enjoy a picnic and take a later train home. Another route goes to Lemont at the base of Mount Nittany, and a final route travels to Julian, which is home to a gliderport from which sailplanes have set world endurance records.

Because the Bellefonte Historical Railroad uses rail diesel cars, the rides are smooth and relaxing, and they're most spectacular in October, when the leaves change colors.

The Region: Bellefonte is the county seat of Centre County. It's a Victorian town dominated by steep hills, and once it was the most important and famous town in the county. Today, that distinction belongs to State College, about 10 miles to the south and the home of Penn State University.

The easiest way to explore and learn about Bellefonte is to take the walking tour, which begins at the railroad station, where maps are available. The tour contains 45 stops, including many beautiful and large buildings, such as the Brockerhoff Hotel, an 1860s Gothic-Revival structure.

Centre County, named for its location, is a lightly populated mountainous area. Between many of the steep mountains are fertile valleys where Plain Sect (Amish and Mennonite) farmers work the soil.

The biggest events in Centre County are Penn State football games. If you're coming to ride the train on a Saturday when the Nittany Lions are playing at home, you'll be wise to avoid driving anywhere near State College, and your chances of finding a motel room anywhere in the county are poor. That doesn't mean that you shouldn't come to ride the train, but leave early and make sure that you have reservations if you plan to stay overnight in the area.

Picture Taking: Along Spring Creek in Milesburg or at the station

Schedule: The basic schedule is Saturdays and Sundays at 1 and 3 P.M. from May through October.

Special Events: Dinner trains operate the last Friday of each month from January through October. The Santa Claus

Express operates on weekends in December and features a visit from Santa Claus and a stop at a Nativity scene.

Fares: Adults are $6.00 and children (3 to 11) are $3.00.

Power: Unique among Pennsylvania tourist railroads, the Bellefonte Historical operates rail diesel cars. These are commuter rail cars with their own diesel power sources.

Nearby Attractions: Victorian Bellefonte; Curtin Village; Penn's Cave; Shaver's Creek Environmental Center; Penn State football

Tourist Information: Centre County Lion Country Convention and Visitors Bureau, 1402 S. Atherton St., State College, PA 16801, telephone 800-358-5466

Nearest Tourist Railroad: East Broad Top—66 miles away

Corry—New York & Lake Erie Railroad, Erie Limited

Telephone: 716-532-5716

Location and Directions: Corry is in Erie County, about 30 miles southeast of Lake Erie. The depot is on Center Street, at the intersection of PA 426 and PA 77.

Now and Then: The Erie Limited is part of the New York & Lake Erie Railroad, based in Gowanda, New York. During the week, the line carries freight. In Corry, the tracks of the NY & LE lie right beside the tracks of the Allegheny Railroad, another short-line freight hauler. The NY & LE was originally part of the Erie Railroad. Later it became part of the Erie Lackawanna Railroad.

The Station: Built in 1951, the Corry depot is one of the youngest railroad depots in the state. It was originally a stop on the Erie Railroad. Today it houses the ticket booth and souvenir shop.

The Route: Leaving from Corry, the line goes southwest to Cambridge Springs, following French Creek for most of its route.

Approximate Trip Time: Three hours

New York & Lake Erie Railroad: this powerful diesel locomotive and welded rail allow the New York & Lake Erie to attain the highest speed of any of Pennsylvania's tourist railroads.

The station in Corry is pleasant and modern, built in 1951.

The Ride: The Erie Limited runs by benefit of welded rails, so it can attain much higher speeds than most other tourist railroads. Legally, the train may go as fast as 60 MPH, but the operators don't try to attain that speed. The regular operating range is 30 to 35 MPH, and an electronic speedometer in the observation car tells the current speed. The passenger cars are from the 1950s, and the observation car gives a great view of where the train has just been. An Amtrak lounge car provides nourishment for the trip.

Much of the region between Corry and Cambridge Springs is swampland. For most of its route, the Erie Limited runs through sparsely populated areas beside French Creek. In some places, large potato farms operate beside the line, and in other regions the track is the high ground through the swamp. The line passes through a few small towns and some of the industries served by the freight line. In Cambridge Springs, passengers have a layover while the train moves down the tracks to turn around. A sign indicates that the town is exactly halfway between New York and Chicago. Passengers have enough time to eat or to walk around, and the local fire house makes its restrooms available for train passengers.

The Region: Corry was once a big railroad town. The town's growth began in the 1860s when the Atlantic and Great Western Railroad intersected the Erie and Sunbury Railroad. One large railroad manufacturer in Corry was the Climax Locomotive Company, which made engines used in the timber industry. A Climax locomotive is now on display at the Corry Area Historical Society. Today Corry is a manufacturing city with diverse industries.

Cambridge Springs grew up from the popularity of mineral water therapy in the late 19th century. At one time as many as 40 hotels housed visitors who came to bathe in the healing waters. Today only one hotel still operates. The Riverside Inn is just a short walk from the spot where passengers leave the train to wait for it to turn around.

Topographically, Erie County is different from surrounding

regions. It's flatter and swampier that most of the rest of Pennsylvania.

Picture Taking: At the station in Corry or on Route 8 in Union City

Schedule: The trains run Saturdays and Sundays from Memorial Day through October, with departures at 1 P.M. from Corry.

Fares: Adults are $10.00 and children (3 to 11) are $5.00.

Power: Diesel

Special Events: Easter, Fall Foliage

Nearby Attractions: Lake Erie; Allegheny National Forest

Tourist Information: Crawford County Tourist Promotion Agency, 881 Water St., Meadville, PA 16335, telephone 800-332-2338; Erie Area Conventions and Visitors Bureau, 1006 State St., Erie, PA 16501, telephone 814-454-7191, e-mail address Erie-chamber@erie.net

Nearest Tourist Railroad: Oil Creek & Titusville—30 miles away

Marienville and Kane—Knox & Kane Railroad

Telephone: 814-927-6621

Location and Directions: The train makes one trip a day. You can board in either Marienville, for the 8-hour ride, or in Kane—which is the only stop between Marienville and the train's destination, the Kinzua Bridge—for the 3½-hour ride. The station in Marienville is one block east of Route 66. Look for the sign in the center of town. The loading area in Kane is a ticket booth beside Kane High School. To reach it, turn south on Route 321 on the east side of Kane.

Now and Then: The Knox & Kane Railroad carries only tourist traffic between Marienville and the Kinzua Bridge. The first rail line through Kane opened in 1864 as part of the Philadelphia and Erie Railroad. Kane was the highest point on that line. Kinzua Bridge, which was not on the first line, was built in 1882, and then replaced in 1900.

Knox & Kane Railroad.

The Station: The station in Marienville is an authentic railroad station with a ticket booth and a waiting room. Many trains are on the tracks there. In Kane, the loading area is just a parking lot and a ticket booth.

The Route: The line parallels PA 66 from Marienville to Kane, traveling through dense woods and crossing the highway several times. Leaving Kane, the line parallels U.S. 6 for several miles before heading into the woods for the final five miles of the journey.

Approximate Trip Time: Eight hours (from Marienville—96 miles) or three and a half hours (from Kane—32 miles)

The Ride: Don't look down if heights scare you. The highlight of a ride on the Knox & Kane is truly a highlight. The Kinzua Bridge is very long and high above the creek, and it stops in the middle of the bridge to give you a good look down. For those who get weak in the knees, the train stops to give passengers a chance to get off before they cross the bridge.

After the train crosses the bridge, it stops for lunch and

The Knox & Kane steams out of Kane and heads for the Kinzua Bridge.

The train passes over the tracks of the Buffalo and Pittsburgh Railroad near the boarding area in Kane.

pictures, and for the engine to turn around. (Lunches are available for $3.75 but must be ordered in advance. There is a covered pavillion at the picnic site.) The truly adventurous can hike down to the creek to get some good pictures of the bridge, but don't attempt this if you aren't in good shape or you don't have the right shoes. The trail is steep and rocky, but it does offer some great photo opportunities. Everyone can walk across the bridge, however.

From Marienville to Kane, the line travels through the Allegheny National Forest. The rail line runs close to PA Route 66 and crosses that road several times. From Kane to the end of the line, the train moves through fields, back yards, and even a golf course. Between Kane and Mount Jewett, the rail line runs close to U.S. Route 6. The ride is scenic and relaxing, but it's the bridge that provides the real excitement on the Knox & Kane.

Kinzua Bridge, built in 1882, was at that time the highest railroad bridge in the world. Today it's fourth in the world and second in the United States. Rebuilt in 1900 to handle heavier traffic, the bridge is 2,053 feet long. One curiosity surrounding the bridge is that the area from Kane to the bridge is only moderately hilly; then, the earth just seems to fall away. The Kinzua Creek, which is the body of water beneath the bridge, is a small stream, shallow and just a few feet wide. It doesn't look like a stream that could cut a 301-foot deep gorge in the earth, but that's what it's done.

The Region: Marienville lies in Forest County, Pennsylvania's least densely populated county, with only about 5,000 residents. Most of the region is still in forest, and the area is extremely popular with outdoor lovers. Nearly half of the 428 square mile county is publicly owned. The Allegheny National Forest, Pennsylvania's only national forest, covers 512,000 acres, and more than 300 species of wildlife inhabit the forest. Among them are white-tail deer, black bears, red foxes, porcupines, weasels, and birds of prey.

Forest County prides itself on what it doesn't have—there

are no traffic lights, no four-lane highways, no radio stations, and no daily newspapers. The train also travels through Elk and McKean counties, and they have slightly more development, although they're both lightly populated and heavily forested.

Oil and timber were the area's initial economic attractions. The world's first oil well is less than 100 miles to the west, and oil rigs are still visible throughout the region. Kane, which is in McKean County, calls itself "The Black Cherry Capital of the World." Black cherry trees provide prized lumber, and a single tree can be worth as much as $6,000.

Marienville is a tiny place, and if you stay there to catch the early train, you can find comfortable lodging, food, gasoline, and ATM machines.

Kane is a pleasant little town where cars stop at painted crosswalks to let pedestrians cross the street; it has a population of only about 4,600. But it is considerably bigger than Marienville, and boasts two famous sports figures—professional and Olympic basketball coach Chuck Daly and 1996 Olympic 5,000-meter runner Amy Rudolph. Signs commemorating their achievements are all over town.

This isn't a warm-weather site, and in winter, Kane and nearby Bradford often show up at the bottom of the temperature list for Pennsylvania and even for the entire country. Summers are warm, but measurably cooler than in other parts of Pennsylvania.

Picture Taking: Many. For photographers, a good strategy is to leave Marienville when the train does and drive to Kane. The train runs beside Route 66 in many places and crosses the road several times. You can also take pictures along Route 6 east of Kane, and at Kinzua Bridge State Park. One of the best spots is close to the loading area in Kane. There, two rail lines cross, and you may be able to get a shot of one train passing over another.

Schedule: Trains leave Marienville at 8:30 A.M. and Kane at 10:45 A.M.

June, September—Friday, Saturday, Sunday

July, August—Tuesday through Sunday

October—Wednesday through Sunday (first two weeks); Saturday, Sunday (second two weeks)

Special Events: None

Fares: From Marienville

Adults	$20.00
Children 3 to 12	$13.00
From Kane	
Adults	$14.00
Children 3 to 12	$8.00

Power: Steam (the trains were built in China in the 1980s)

Nearby Attractions: Allegheny National Forest; Kinzua Dam

Tourist Information: Elk County Visitors Bureau, P.O. Box 838, Saint Mary's, PA 18537, telephone 814-834-3723; Forest County Tourist Promotion Agency, P.O. Box 608, Tionesta, PA 16353, telephone 800-222-1706 (in PA) or 814-927-8266; Seneca Highlands Tourist Association (McKean County), 10 E. Warren Rd., Custer City, PA 16725, telephone 814-368-9370

Nearest Tourist Railroad: Oil Creek & Titusville—42 miles from Marienville, 66 miles from Kane

Titusville—Oil Creek & Titusville Railroad

Telephone: 814-676-1733

Location and Directions: Titusville is in northwestern Pennsylvania. The biggest road into town is PA Route 8, which originates in Pittsburgh and runs north to Erie. Because of the mountains in the area, no major east-west route goes into Titusville.

The train station is at 409 S. Perry St. in downtown Titusville. Perry Street is Truck Route 8. To board at Drake Well Museum, take PA Route 8, and turn east on Bloss Street on the south side of Titusville, just south of Oil Creek. It's just over a mile to the museum.

Now and Then: Both passengers and freight travel on the OC & T, which is owned by the New York & Lake Erie Railroad

Oil Creek & Titusville Railroad.

Perry Street Station in downtown Titusville is the headquarters of the Oil Creek & Titusville Railroad.

of Gowanda, New York. The line has been operating since the 1880s.

The Station: Perry Street Station is a renovated freight station that has a ticket booth, a dining area, and a souvenir shop.

The Route: The train winds through Titusville for about two miles. Then it parallels Oil Creek for the rest of the route to Rynd Farm.

Approximate Trip Time: Two and a half hours

The Ride: From the Perry Street Station in Titusville, the train rolls through the small city for just a few minutes. As soon as the train gets warmed up, it stops at Drake Well Museum, the place where the oil boom began. Riders may board and depart there.

On the train, the favorite spot for riders is an open-air gondola car that's at the back end of the train going in one direction and directly behind the engine going in the other direction. It's not the most luxurious car in the train business. It has no chairs or benches, but it's a pleasant place to take in the scenery. Riders in the open car can enjoy the fresh air, and they can see, hear, and smell the engine. This car can also serve bicyclists and canoeists. They can either ride or paddle south and then take the train back north. Oil Creek is popular with canoeists, and a paved bike path runs beside the creek.

At Rynd Farm, the southern end of the ride, the train stops, and the engine moves from one end of the train to the other for the return trip. Passengers can get off the train for about 20 minutes, and snacks and souvenirs are available.

A favorite feature of the OC & T is the Railway Postal Car. It's the only working Railway Postal Car in the United States, and you can send postcards and have them canceled and sorted as you watch.

Train riders frequently spot deer, blue herons, and even bald eagles along the water, and the creek is a favorite among trout and bass fishermen.

The Region: You may never have heard of Oil Creek or Titusville, but something that happened here over 135 years ago has a tremendous impact on every part of your life.

Many regions like to exaggerate slightly the importance of events in their history, but events in the Oil Creek Valley truly were significant in shaping the world that we live in today. In 1858 and 1859, Edwin Drake, known as "Colonel," drilled for oil beside Oil Creek. On August 28, 1859, his drilling finally paid off and resulted in the world's first oil well. After that, the valley boomed briefly, but the oil deposits proved to be rather modest. Today, a small amount of oil still comes out of the ground in northwestern Pennsylvania, but the region bears no resemblance to Saudi Arabia.

Instead, the entire region is largely forest, and the train runs through woods along Oil Creek, with steep hills rising on both sides. From the train windows, you can see many remnants of the oil boom. The major one is the Drake Well Museum on the site of the first successful well. At the museum, you can learn about the earliest days of the oil industry.

The oil boom resulted in tremendous environmental degradation to the area. Drillers cut down every tree on many hillsides, and huge quantities of oil spilled into the water. Today, however, the earth has recovered, and in summer all is green.

Picture Taking: At Perry Street Station and at Drake Well Museum

Schedule: Regular season is mid-June to mid-October. Extra Fall Foliage trains run in October. All trains leave Drake Well Park 15 minutes after Perry Street Station, and leave Rynd Farm for the return trip one and a quarter hours after that.

June, September—Saturdays, Sundays: 2 P.M.

July, August, early October—Wednesday through Sunday: 2 P.M.

October—Saturdays and Sundays: 11:45 A.M., 3:15 P.M.; Wednesday, Thursday, Friday: 2 P.M.

Also available during the second and third weeks of May and the first two weeks of October are school runs which leave Perry Street Station at 11:15 A.M. in May and at 10:45 A.M. in October.

Special Events:
Mystery Dinner Excursions—Second, fourth Saturday in July, last Saturday in August, second, fourth Saturday in September at 6:45 P.M.

Moonlight Honky Tonk—Second Saturday in August at 6 P.M.

Peter Cottontail Express—Saturday before Easter at 2 P.M.

Haunted Train—Saturday before Halloween at 6 P.M.

Santa Excursions—Middle weekend in December at 2 P.M.

Fares: There is no extra charge for bicycles or canoes; one-way fares for cyclists or canoeists are $3.00 less than round trips.

Adults	$9.00
Seniors (60 and up)	$8.00
Students 3 to 17	$5.00

Power: Diesel

Nearby Attractions: Drake Well Museum; Oil Creek Bike Trail

Tourist Information: Crawford County Tourist Promotion Agency, 881 Water St., Meadville, PA 16335, telephone 800-332-2338; Venango County Area Tourist Promotion Agency, 213 12th St., Franklin, PA 16323, telephone 800-776-4526

Nearest Tourist Railroad: New York & Lake Erie—30 miles away

The Trolleys

Kempton—Wanamaker, Kempton & Southern Railroad, Berksy Trolley

Telephone: 610-756-6469

Location and Directions: The W, K & S is in northern Berks County, far from any beaten path, in the small town of Kempton. PA routes 143 and 737 run through Kempton. The nearest cities are Reading to the south and Allentown to the east. To get to Kempton, take PA 143 or PA 737 North from U.S. 22/Interstate 78 and look for the signs to the W, K & S.

Most of the time, the W, K & S operates steam train rides. However, on Saturdays in June, September and part of October, the Berksy Trolley runs instead of the train.

Now and Then: The Berksy Trolley is an old brakeman's jitney, converted into a trolley in 1971. It takes its name from the Reading Railroad's local passenger train, which the locals called the "Berksy."

The Station: See entry for Wanamaker, Kempton & Southern Railroad in Southeast chapter

The Route: The Berksy follows the same route as the trains of the W, K & S Railroad. It runs beside Ontaulanee Creek from Kempton to Wanamakers on a portion of the Reading Railroad's Schuylkill and Lehigh branch line. The Blue Mountains stand to the west of the route, and they carry the Appalachian

Trail, which runs from Maine to Georgia, through the region. In Wanamakers, the original railroad station is open as an antique shop on Sundays.

Approximate Trip Time: 35 minutes

The Ride: The Berksy rolls through a lightly populated agricultural valley between Reading and Allentown. Farms and fields surround the line, and steep wooded hillsides are all around. The trolley is small, seating 20 passengers.

The Region: See entry for Wanamaker, Kempton & Southern Railroad in Southeast chapter

Picture Taking: Along PA Route 143 south of Wanamakers

Schedule: June, September, first week in October—Saturday: 1, 2, 3, 4 P.M.

Special Events: None

Fares: Adults are $4.50 and children 3 to 11 are $2.50.

Power: Self-powered by electric motor

Nearby Attractions: Hawk Mountain; Lehigh County Velodrome

Tourist Information: Reading and Berks County Visitors Bureau, P.O. Box 6627, Reading, PA 19610, telephone 800-443-6610; or Lehigh Valley Convention and Visitors Bureau, P.O. Box 20785, Lehigh Valley, PA 18002-0785, telephone 800-747-0561

Nearest Tourist Railroad: Wanamaker, Kempton & Southern—same; East Penn—17 miles away

Philadelphia—Welcome Line Trolley

Telephone: 215-580-7800

Location and Directions: The primary route runs on 11th and 12th Streets, beginning at the Reading Terminal Market on 12th, just north of Market.

At different times during the year, historic trolleys run in and around Philadelphia. If you want to ride one, be sure to call ahead to find out if any are running. SEPTA, the regional transportation authority, is responsible for operating the trolleys.

The Welcome Line Trolley stops beside the Reading Terminal Market.

Advocates of mass transportation are working to restore trolley service, and the tourist runs serve as promotional vehicles.

Now and Then: The trolleys appear only for tourist runs during holiday seasons and for special occasions. Trolley tracks are still in place on many streets, and some advocates are trying to return regular trolley service to the city. In times past, however, streetcars carried thousands of passengers around Philadelphia and its suburbs every day. The trolleys went into practically every city neighborhood and ran continuously all day and most of the night.

The Route: The Welcome Line Trolley begins its run at the Reading Terminal Market on 12th Street. It proceeds south to Fitzwater Street, east to 11th, north to Noble, west to 12th, and back to the Reading Terminal Market on 11th.

Approximate Trip Time: The two-and-a-half mile route takes about 20 minutes, although traffic and traffic lights can lengthen the ride.

The Ride: One route used during the Christmas season runs about 2 miles through Center City. It begins at the Reading Terminal Market on 12th, just north of Market, goes south for about a mile, heads over to 11th, then heads back north. The line runs through heavy city traffic, and it lets riders know how hundreds of thousands of Philadelphians used to travel around their city. Other areas where trolleys run periodically are Germantown and Media. On a regular basis, streetcars operate throughout the city and suburbs on the Subway and the El—the elevated rail lines.

The Region: Philadelphia is the biggest city in Pennsylvania. It's home to Independence Hall, the Liberty Bell, the Betsy Ross House, the Italian Market, and many more attractions. You can tour the city by boat, bus, foot, and car.

Picture Taking: Anywhere along the line

Schedule: No set schedule. Call for information.

Special Events: The Welcome Line Trolley operates during the Christmas season from the day after Thanksgiving until the Saturday before New Year's Day. It also operates at other times during the year when the tourist bureau decides to run it. Call before heading to Philadelphia.

Fares: Holiday trolleys are free. Regular transit fare is $1.60.

Power: Electric

Nearby Attractions: Transit Museum (see Museums chapter); Independence Hall; Liberty Bell; Veterans Stadium; Italian Market; Penn's Landing; Saint Joseph's University; the Palestra

Tourist Information: Philadelphia Convention and Visitors Bureau. 16th St. and JFK Boulevard, Philadelphia, PA 19102, telephone 215-636-1666

Nearest Tourist Railroads: Brandywine Scenic; New Hope & Ivyland—both about 35 miles away

Rockhill Furnace—Shade Gap Electric Railway

Telephone: 814-447-9576

Location and Directions: The Rockhill Trolley Museum, where the trolley is located, is adjacent to the East Broad Top

Riders on the Shade Gap Electric Railway can enjoy the summer air.

Railroad in Huntingdon County. Rockhill is in south central Pennsylvania, about 110 miles southeast of Pittsburgh. From east or west, take the Pennsylvania Turnpike to exit 13, Fort Littleton. Go north on U.S. 522. Orbisonia is 19 miles north of the turnpike.

Now and Then: No trolleys actually worked on this line, which was a part of the East Broad Top Railroad during its days as a working freight and passenger railroad. The trolleys have come from different parts of the world, such as Argentina, to reside in the museum and to carry passengers on a short journey.

The Station: The trolleys leave from a platform across the street from the East Broad Top Railroad.

The Route: The trolleys travel through the repair yard, past the trolley barn, and into the woods for their short three-mile runs. Along the route, passengers can see remnants of coal mining operations and an iron forge.

Approximate Trip Time: 20 minutes

The Ride: The Rockhill Trolley Museum (see Museums

chapter) restores and operates streetcars for a ride on a short stretch of track called the Shade Gap Electric Railway that goes in the opposite direction from the East Broad Top Railroad. You can ride both the train and the trolley on the same day. The trolley ride is shorter than the train ride, and the conductors and engineers try to time the rides so that it's possible to do both without much of a wait.

The museum has a collection of cars and rotates them throughout the year. In summer a completely open car that originally ran in South America provides a comfortable ride. The trolleys run on a one-mile stretch of track that was a part of the East Broad Top Railroad. It's a heavily wooded corridor and many parts of the original railroad infrastructure are visible.

The Region: See entry for East Broad Top in Southwest chapter

Picture Taking: The best shots are available in the train yard.

Schedule: Weekends from Memorial Day through October, on the half-hour from 11:30 A.M. to 4:30 P.M.

Special Events: None

Fares: $4, which includes museum admission

Power: Electric motors

Nearby Attractions: Raystown Lake

Tourist Information: Raystown Country Visitors Bureau, 241 Mifflin St., Huntingdon, PA 16652, telephone 800-269-4696, web site http://www.raystown.org

Nearest Tourist Railroad: East Broad Top, Orbisonia—same location; Bellefonte Historical—66 miles away

Washington—Pennsylvania Trolley Museum

Telephone: 412-228-9256

Location and Directions: Washington is about 25 miles southwest of Pittsburgh on Interstate 79. From I-79, take exit 8 and follow the signs to the Trolley Museum. Be sure to follow the signs closely.

Now and Then: The Pennsylvania Trolley Museum celebrates the history of the streetcars that were America's first form of mass transit in the cities. The museum has a large collection of trolleys from different parts of the country, including a Red Arrow car from Philadelphia, and Car No. 832, the "Streetcar Named Desire" from New Orleans.

The Station: Outside the museum is a small ticket booth reminiscent of those in small towns along trolley lines.

The Route: The trolleys travel on a three-mile route through meadows and woods.

Approximate Trip Time: 30 minutes

The Ride: The trolleys run on about three miles of track laid by volunteers. The route goes through meadows and woods to a turnaround. The bell clangs and the powerful electric motor roars as the car heads out of the station.

The Region: Linked by I-79 to Pittsburgh, Washington is part of the Pittsburgh metropolitan area, but it has its own identity and small town atmosphere. Like much of western Pennsylvania, it has a mining history that includes coal, natural gas, petroleum, clay, and sand.

Covered bridges are one of the county's attraction. The current count of 25 ranks Washington County second in the state, behind only Lancaster County.

Picture Taking: At the station

Schedule: The trolleys run all day while the museum is open (see Museums chapter), but on an informal schedule. The route is only about three miles, so it's never more than 30 minutes between rides.

Special Events:

Trolley Fair (includes a parade, an antique vehicle display, hand car and caboose rides, and model train exhibits)—last weekend in June

County Fair (the Washington County Fairgrounds are close to the museum, and visitors can enjoy the old-fashioned custom of riding a trolley to the fair)—third week in August

Santa Trolley (children can meet Santa on the trolley, and

adults can sing carols, and everyone will enjoy a Lionel toy train layout)—after Thanksgiving

Trolleys and Toy Trains (visitors can enjoy rides on decorated trolleys and the Lionel toy train layout)—December

Fares:

Adults	$5.00
Seniors (65 and up)	$4.00
Children 2 to 11	$3.00

Power: Electric

Nearby Attractions: The Meadows Race Track; Washington County Fairgrounds; Washington County covered bridges (25)

Tourist Information: Washington County Tourism, 59 N. Main St., Washington, PA 15301, telephone 412-222-8130

Nearest Tourist Railroad: Laurel Highlands—49 miles away

The Coal Mines

One of the primary reasons for the construction of railroads in Pennsylvania was to move coal from the mines to the consumers. Pennsylvania has huge coal deposits, and to many Pennsylvanians, the northeastern part of the state is "the Coal Regions." The coal, however, lies in many parts of the state.

While the railroads transported huge amounts of coal from the mines, much smaller rail operations moved coal out of the mines and men into and out of the mines. These railroads had small cars and no creature comforts, and today several of them operate as tourist attractions. A ride into a coal mine won't give you the same look at the world as a ride through the verdant countryside in a regular passenger car, but a ride into a coal mine does offer a fascinating look at a very hard and dangerous occupation.

As the "lokie" enters the mine, all natural light ends. A lokie is a small locomotive that worked in and around coal mines. It's built low to the ground because the ceilings in coal mines were never high. Miners riding to their destinations in the little cars had to keep their heads down or lose them.

A coal mine is a dark and foreboding place, and it's always cool and damp. Even on hot summer days, a mine is chilly, so cover up. If you forget to bring a jacket, the mines usually have coats that you can borrow.

While the rides into coal mines are short, they do provide an excellent educational experience. At one time, coal was king in many parts of Pennsylvania, and these four rides offer an insight into the daily life of a miner, both from the past and the present.

Ashland—Pioneer Tunnel Coal Mine

Telephone: 717-875-3850

Location and Directions: The Pioneer Tunnel Coal Mine is at the top of the town. From Interstate 81, take exit 36W. Take PA 61 N to Ashland. Signs point to the mine, which is at 19th and Oak streets.

Now and Then: The Pioneer Tunnel is an excellent place to get a feel for the life of a coal miner and his family in the 19th century. Miners often worked 12 hours a day, 6 days a week. Pay was low, work was brutal, and the coal companies owned the towns where the miners lived and worked. Adjacent to the Pioneer Tunnel Mine is the Museum of Anthracite Mining, which documents the lives of the early miners in the region.

The hardship of miners' lives inspired the rise of the Molly Maguires, a secret terrorist society that operated in the anthracite region from the mid-1860s to the late 1870s. The largely Irish-American organization attempted to improve living and working conditions in the mining industry.

To achieve these goals, the "Mollies" intimidated and murdered mine owners and superintendents, police officers, and judges. They also initiated several coal strikes, and formed a union. In 1874, Pinkerton detectives were hired to infiltrate the group, which was crushed by a series of murder convictions between 1875 and 1878. The movie *The Molly Maguires* was filmed at Eckley Miners Village in neighboring Luzerne County.

Approximate Trip Time: The mine tour lasts 35 minutes and the train trip around the mountain 30 minutes.

The Ride: Pioneer Tunnel offers two separate rides. One goes into the mine, and the other is a steam train ride behind

A lokie takes visitors hundreds of feet into the earth in the Pioneer Tunnel Coal Mine.

the Henry Clay steam locomotive that takes a ¾ mile route around Mahanoy (not Mahoney) Mountain.

The Region: Coal defines Schuylkill County, and on the ridge visible from the Pioneer Tunnel is the town of Centralia. In 1962, an underground mine fire broke out there. The fire has been burning ever since, and it will burn until it exhausts all the coal in the vein. Since the fire broke out, Centralia has become a ghost town as the residents have relocated.

Picture Taking: Before you board the train

Schedule: The mine is open from May through October. Tours operate on weekends in May, September and October, and every day during the summer. Two rides are available—the mine tour and a ride around the top of a mountain on a lokie, a small steam-powered train. Both rides depart approximately every 45 minutes, from 10 A.M. to 5:30 P.M. (last Lokie ride) or 6 P.M. (last mine tour). But the schedule isn't strict; the operators will hold rides to accommodate visitors. Group tours are available during the off-season with prior reservations.

Special Events: None

Fares: Mine Tour

    Adults $5.00

    Children under 12 $3.00

                 Train Ride

    Adults $2.50

    Children under 12 $2.50

Power: The "lokie" runs on steam power. The small train that travels inside the mine runs on battery power.

Nearby Attractions: Museum of Anthracite Mining (adjacent to mine); Yuengling's in Pottsville (America's oldest brewery); Hawk Mountain, Knoebels Grove Amusement Park

Tourist Information: Schuylkill County Visitors Bureau, 91 S. Progress Ave., Pottsville, PA 17901, telephone 800-765-7282

Nearest Tourist Railroad: West Shore—40 miles away

Patton—Seldom Seen Mine

Telephone: 800-237-8590 or 814-247-6305 (in season)

Location and Directions: The mine is on PA Route 36, four miles north of Patton. The nearest big city is Johnstown. The nearest major highway is U.S. 22.

Now and Then: The Seldom Seen Mine is an example of a small, family-owned mining operation. The Radomsky family operated the mine from 1910 to 1960, and after it closed down it became a tourist attraction.

Approximate Trip Time: One hour

The Ride: The tram heads into the mine and travels deep underground, where miners once dug coal by hand. The atmosphere is cool and damp, and it can be somewhat scary. The work in the mine was grueling, and the pay was low, sometimes as little as 25 cents a ton. Many of the guides are former miners, and they can describe the rigors of spending their working lives in such an environment.

The Region: Seldom Seen Mine is in Cambria County, which is also home to the Johnstown Incline (see Inclines chapter), the Allegheny Portage Railroad National Historic Site (see Museums chapter), and the Station Inn (see Resting chapter). Small towns and steep mountains define the area. Patton is one of those small towns. Many visitors come to Prince Gallitzin State Park for camping, boating, fishing, and picnicking.

Coal was one of the dominant forces that shaped this region, but the coal industry has shrunk considerably over the last four decades. As you drive through, you can see many remnants of coal's boom days, from mines to breakers. Throughout the region are many natural wonders, such as the Conemaugh Gap, a 1,350-foot deep gorge visible from a scenic overlook along Route 56 west of Johnstown.

Picture Taking: Before you board the train

Schedule:

June, September—Saturday, Sunday: 12 noon to 6 P.M.

July, August—Thursday to Sunday: 12 noon to 6 P.M.

Memorial Day weekend, July 4, Labor Day: 12 noon to 6 P.M.

Special Events: Haunted Mine Tours—two weekends prior to Halloween

Fares: Adults are $5.00 and children under 12 are $3.00.

Power: Battery power

Nearby Attractions: Johnstown Incline (see Inclines chapter); Horseshoe Curve; Ghost Town Trail; Allegheny Portage Railroad (see Museums chapter)

Tourist Information: Cambria County Tourist Council, 111 Market St., Johnstown, PA 15901, telephone 814-536-7993

Nearest Tourist Railroad: Amtrak—31 miles away

Scranton—Lackawanna Coal Mine

Telephone: 800-238-7245 or 717-963-MINE

Location and Directions: The mine is in McDade Park in Scranton. From Interstate 81, take exit 57B (Scranton Expressway). Exit at Keyser Avenue South and follow signs to McDade Park. Or, take exit 38 of the Northeast Extension of the Pennsylvania turnpike to Keyser Avenue and follow the signs.

Now and Then: In addition to Lackawanna Coal Mine and a souvenir shop, McDade Park is home to the Pennsylvania Anthracite Museum, with a library and archives. The park has picnic facilities, swimming, and is the site of the Pennsylvania Summer Theater Festival.

Approximate Trip Time: One hour

The Ride: The ride takes visitors 300 feet below the surface of the earth to a place where miners once worked on their hands and knees to dig out the anthracite coal that heated America and fueled industries. The mine is narrow and cool, and the working conditions were hardly pleasant.

The Region: Coal made Scranton the biggest city in northeastern Pennsylvania, and railroads were developed to carry the coal to its markets. Coal and related industries made many millionaires in Scranton, but as coal diminished in importance, the region's economy changed. Today, Scranton is a city with a diverse economy. It's a working-class city with many small manufacturers and service businesses.

Scranton lies in a valley, and mountains rise steeply on the east and west. A ski resort is less than four miles from downtown, and the mountains are home to many types of outdoor activities. At the southern end of the valley is the city of Wilkes-Barre, another city built on coal mining. Writers and speakers often refer to the "Scranton/Wilkes-Barre Area," but the cities are distinct and friendly rivals in many ways.

Picture Taking: Before you board the train

Schedule: The frequency of tours varies according to how busy the site is. More than one tour can operate at the same time, so tours may leave every 20 or 30 minutes. Tours are given during the park's opening hours, April through November, daily from 10:00 A.M. to 4:30 P.M.

Special Events: None involving the mine tour, but McDade Park has Scranton Public Theatre performances during the summer

Fares: Adults are $5.00 and children (3 to 12) are $3.00.

Power: Battery power

Nearby Attractions: Pennsylvania Anthracite Heritage Museum (adjacent); Steamtown National Historic Site (see Museums chapter); Scranton Iron Furnaces; Lackawanna County Stadium (AAA baseball); Pocono downs (harness racing); Pocono Raceway (auto racing)

Tourist Information: Pennsylvania's Northeast Territory Visitors Bureau, 201 Hangar Rd., Suite 203, Avoca, PA 18641, telephone 800-22-WELCOME, web site http://www.travelfile.com

Nearest Tourist Railroad: Steamtown Historic Site—three miles away

Tarentum—Tour-Ed Mine

Telephone: 412-224-4720

Location and Directions: The mine is northeast of Pittsburgh, just off PA Route 28 (Allegheny Valley Expressway).

Now and Then: In addition to the mine, the site contains a 1785 log house, company stores and houses, a strip mine operation, a saw mill, and a mine museum.

Approximate Trip Time: 30 minutes

The Ride: The tram goes deep into the mine, allowing visitors to get an idea of the difficulty and danger involved in bringing coal out of the earth. The roof is no more than seven feet high, and the tunnels through which the tram passes are often quite narrow. Demonstrations show how miners did all work by hand when mining began in the region around 1800, and how they later used machinery which made the work somewhat less strenuous, though hardly easy. Visitors can get out of the cars and walk around.

The Region: Tarentum is part of the Pittsburgh metropolitan area. A century ago, coal mining and steel manufacturing dominated the landscape. Unlike the coal mined in Ashland and Scranton, the coal from Tour-Ed was bituminous, or soft, coal.

Picture Taking: Before you board the train

Schedule: Tours leave when the mine cars are full or close to full. The mine is open Memorial Day through Labor Day, daily (except Tuesday) from 1 to 4 P.M.

Special Events: Antique Flea Market, third Sunday of May, June, July, August, and September, at the miner's village

Fares: Adults are $6.00 and children (3 to 12) are $3.00.

Power: Battery-powered mine motors

Nearby Attractions: Pittsburgh Inclines (see Inclines chapter); Pennsylvania Trolley Museum (see Museums chapter)

Tourist Information: Greater Pittsburgh Convention and Visitors Bureau, 4 Gateway Center, Pittsburgh, PA 15222, telephone 800-366-0093

Nearest Tourist Railroad: Pittsburgh Inclines—16 miles away

The Inclined Railroads

The shortest distance between two points is a straight line, and in many places around the world that simple fact has led to the construction of inclines to carry people from the bottom to the top of a hill. Inclines and variations on them are common in ski resorts, but long before ski resorts existed, "inclines" referred to something quite different, which served a more utilitarian function. Essentially, they were trolley cars that ran almost directly up the side of a hill or mountain on steel cables, powered by electricity.

Today, three inclines are still operating in Pennsylvania, and the one in Johnstown claims the distinction of being the steepest inclined plane railway in the world—71.9 degrees. In Pittsburgh, two inclines are still working, but a century ago that city boasted fifteen.

Riding an incline is different from riding a more traditional railroad: an incline is more likely to give you a funny feeling in your stomach. The ride is definitely a memorable experience, as is the view from the top.

Johnstown—Johnstown Incline

Telephone: 814-536-1816

Location and Directions: Johnstown is in southwestern Pennsylvania, about 30 miles northwest of the PA Turnpike. Take the

The Johnstown Incline, the world's steepest incline, carries passengers and cars.

Bedford exit and go northwest on PA 56 right into Johnstown. The incline is easy to spot from anywhere in Johnstown. It's accessible from Routes 56/403, Roosevelt Boulevard in downtown, and off PA 271, Menoher Boulevard on Edgehill Drive in Westmont. It's also easy to walk to the incline from downtown. An elevated walkway carries pedestrians safely across the busy highway.

Now and Then: After the flood of 1889 (see Amtrak-Horseshoe Curve entry in Southwest chapter), the Cambria Iron Company decided to put a new suburb called Westmont on top of the hill overlooking the city, out of the way of subsequent floods. To reach Westmont, they built the Johnstown Inclined Plane, which opened in 1891. The incline runs right up the side of the hill, climbing 634 feet at a grade of 71.9 degrees, making it the steepest vehicular inclined plane in the world, according to the Guiness Book of World Records.

Before individual ownership of automobiles became common, the incline was primarily a local form of mass transportation. It still serves that purpose on a small scale, but its bigger attraction is to tourists. Visitors can dine in the restaurant at the top and watch a baseball or football game in Point Stadium below, although it's difficult to follow the intricacies of a game from such a height. There are also a souvenir and snack shop, a museum, a park, and a hiking trail.

The Ride: On a clear day, it's easy to see how Johnstown became the victim of a flood. The city itself lies at the confluence of several streams, with hills rising steeply on all sides. On a cloudy day, you can literally rise into the clouds.

The Region: Johnstown's lasting fame came from the flood of 1889, but before and after that disaster, Johnstown was a prosperous city whose economy centered on steel, coal, and the railroad. The completion of Horseshoe Curve in 1854 opened up the western half of Pennsylvania to development. Until then, the Allegheny Mountains had been an almost insurmountable obstacle to westward expansion. Johnstown lies about 15 miles west of the crest of the Alleghenies.

Picture Taking: The observation deck on top of the hill is good. For unusual shots of the undersides of cars, take the hiking trail which winds between the top station and the bottom station.

Schedule: Every 15 minutes, 7 a.m. to midnight, 7 days a week

Special Events: Laser light shows take place on weekend nights, creating changing light sculptures in the sky.

Fares: $1.00

Power: Electric

Nearby Attractions: Johnstown Flood Museum

Tourist Information: Cambria County Tourist Council, 111 Market St., Johnstown, PA 15901, telephone 800-237-8590

Nearest Tourist Railroad: Amtrak, Horseshoe Curve—four city blocks away

The Pittsburgh Inclines

The Duquesne Incline and the Monangahela Incline are the only survivors of the 15 inclines that once served the residents of Pittsburgh and its suburbs. Both of these inclines travel up and down Mount Washington, which today is a comfortable residential area but which was once Coal Hill, the home of coal mining operations. It's possible to walk from one to the other. The Duquesne Incline is west of the Monangahela Incline.

When the inclines come down, they're close to the Three Rivers Stadium and the point where the Monangahela and Allegheny rivers merge to form the Ohio. Travel by incline is much quicker than a similar trip by automobile, and the rides offer great views. One part of those views is the freight trains that run almost constantly on the tracks along the river. The clear views of the city that are possible today were rarities 50 and 100 years ago, when the steel industry dominated the city and smoke from hundreds of factories darkened the skies.

Duquesne Incline

Telephone: 412-381-1665

Location and Directions: You can board the Duquesne Incline at either the top or the bottom of its run. The lower station offers free parking. To reach the incline from downtown Pittsburgh, cross the Fort Pitt Bridge and turn right to the lower station. The lower station is very close to the point where the Monangahela and Allegheny rivers join to form the Ohio.

Now and Then: The Duquesne Incline serves both tourist and local residents who can live atop Mount Washington and be in downtown Pittsburgh is less than 10 minutes. At the upper station are an observation deck and a museum that recalls the history of inclines in Pittsburgh and all over the world. Volunteers give narrated tours, explaining the machinery and the history of the operation. The machinery is visible

Duquesne Incline.

A museum at the top station tells the story of inclined railroads.

and you can watch the huge cables and gears as they pull the cars. The Duquesne Incline opened in 1877. It's 800 feet long and it rises 400 feet at an angle of 30 degrees.

The Station: The top station is both a place to board the incline and a place to see how it works. The gears and cables that move the cars are visible, and a small museum about inclines is located there. An adjacent observation deck provides a great view of Pittsburgh and an opportunity to watch the incline's cars as they climb and descend. The bottom station is just a place to enter and depart.

The Ride: Both Pittsburgh inclines go up the side of the same mountain. These inclines opened the Mount Washington section of the city to development and enabled people to live about 600 feet above the downtown area.

The Region: Pittsburgh is a curious place to put a place. The reason for its existence is the confluence of the Monangahela and Allegheny rivers, which meet at the Point and become the Ohio River. Hills rise steeply from the rivers, and half a mile from the center of the city a highway tunnel goes right through a mountain. All over the city, no streets seem to run at 90-degree angles. Just west of the Fort Pitt Tunnel, along the Monangahela River, is the Duquesne Incline.

From the top, you'll have a fantastic view of the city. Below you'll see trains, barges on the rivers, and Three Rivers Stadium. The top station contains waiting rooms, exhibits, and mementos of the incline's past.

Pittsburgh is Pennsylvania's second-largest city, and it's literally not the city that it used to be. Once, steel dominated life and the economy in Pittsburgh. Smoke from factories and foundries filled the sky, and it frequently clouded the view that you can now enjoy from the top stations of the inclines. Today, Pittsburgh's economy is different. The city is primarily service-based, and full of museums and monuments.

Picture Taking: The observation deck at the top and the area outside the bottom station

Schedule: The rides last only about three minutes, and the incline runs continuously. It is open at 6:00 A.M. and runs until 12:45 A.M.

Special Events: None, but volunteers give tours of the upper station at varying times. Call ahead to find out when the tours are available and to make reservations.

Fares: $1.00 each way

Power: Originally steam powered, the Incline now runs on electricity.

Tourist Information: Greater Pittsburgh Convention and Visitors Bureau, 4 Gateway Center, Pittsburgh, PA 15222, telephone 800-366-0093

Nearest Tourist Railroad: Laurel Highlands—41 miles away

Monangahela Incline

Telephone: 412-361-0873

Location and Directions: The lower station is on West Carson Street. The upper station is on Grandview Avenue, Mount Washington. From downtown Pittsburgh, cross the Liberty Bridge. Then turn right on McArdle Roadway and left on Grandview Avenue.

Now and Then: The Monangahela Incline opened in 1870. It travels 635 feet and rises 367 feet at a grade of 35 degrees. Its operating speed is 6 MPH. The Monangahela Incline was so successful that it added a freight incline in 1884 to haul horses, buggies, furniture, and coal. The freight incline survived until 1935.

In 1983, the Incline received a thorough renovation that included new track, ties, and girders and restoration of the stations to their original Victorian atmosphere. In 1994 another restoration brought a new motor generator and braking system.

The Station: The top station is attractive, with some old pictures of the incline and the city. The bottom station is basically just functional.

The Ride: Both Pittsburgh inclines go up the side of the same mountain. These inclines opened the Mount Washington

Monangahela Incline.

section of the city to development and enabled people to live about 600 feet above the downtown area.

The Region: See entry for Duquesne Incline above

Picture Taking: The observation deck at the top and the area outside the bottom station

Schedule: The rides last only about three minutes, and the incline runs continuously from 5:30 A.M. to 12:45 A.M., Monday through Saturday, and 8:45 A.M. to midnight, Sundays and holidays.

Special Events: None

Fares: $1.00 each way

Power: Originally steam powered, the Incline now runs on electricity.

Tourist Information: Greater Pittsburgh Convention and Visitors Bureau, 4 Gateway Center, Pittsburgh, PA 15222, telephone 800-366-0093

Nearest Tourist Railroad: Laurel Highlands—41 miles away

The Museums

These museums fall into two categories—large and small. The former, besides having bigger collections, are open almost every day of the year.

Large Museums

Altoona—Altoona Railroaders Memorial Museum and Horseshoe Curve Visitors Center

Telephone: 814-946-0834

Location and Directions: The museum is in downtown Altoona, at 9th Avenue and 13th Street. From the Pennsylvania Turnpike, take exit 11, Route 220 North to Altoona. From 220, take the 17th Street exit to downtown. Turn right onto 9th Avenue at Station Mall. The museum is adjacent to the mall.

To reach the Horseshoe Curve, follow the Heritage Route Trail signs. Take 9th Avenue to 17th Street and turn left. Then go right on 6th Avenue and follow that to Burgoon Road and turn right. Go left on Beale Avenue and right on 40th Street. Horseshoe Curve is on State Route 4008. The Heritage Route will take you to the Allegheny Portage Railroad National Historic Site.

The Museum's Story: Lying at the base of the mountain range that forms the Eastern Continental Divide, Altoona was once the busiest railroad town in the world. The Pennsylvania

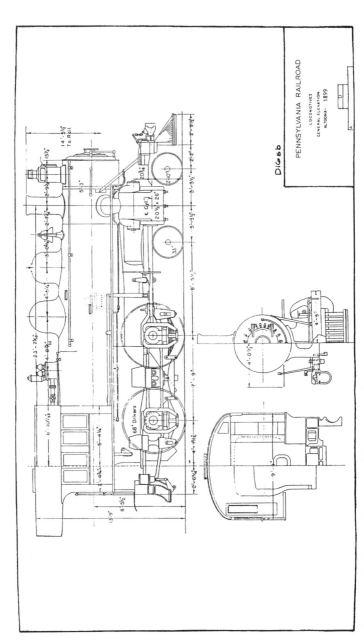

PENNSYLVANIA RAILROAD

LOCOMOTIVES
GENERAL ELEVATION
ALTOONA - 1899

D166b

Courtesy Railroad Museum of Pennsylvania

Railroad's Altoona shops built more than 6,000 locomotives and did most of the maintenance for the rolling stock of the world's most powerful railroad.

This museum focuses on telling the story of the people who worked on the railroad as much as on the trains and the powerful men who ran the corporation. The railroad was the focal point of its workers' lives, and that influence even extended to the custom of Mondays being wash days. Fewer trains operated on Monday, since that was the day when they went in for maintenance and repairs, and thus less coal dust was in the air on Mondays.

Beside the museum is the busy Conrail/Amtrak line that travels through Horseshoe Curve, so you can watch trains almost constantly. Across the tracks is the Altoona Amtrak station, so you can come by train (see Southwest chapter) and walk to the museum.

This museum allows visitors to look at and listen to the lives of railroad workers. Visitors can hear simulated conversations between members of railroad workers' families and listen to radio shows from different periods. The interior look of the house changes periodically to reflect the lives of the different ethnic groups who lived in Altoona and kept the Pennsylvania Railroad running.

In addition to building and maintaining equipment, the railroad had a lab on the grounds. In the lab the railroad tested its heavy equipment, and also tried to figure out how to get the most orange juice out of an orange. For a railroad seeking maximum efficiency, that was an important consideration.

Much of the museum's focus is on the building and use of Horseshoe Curve, and you can also visit the curve by car. A funicular railroad carries visitors to track level to watch trains work their way up the ridge. On a busy day, 50 or more trains pass through the curve. The best time to visit is the latter part of the week. Thursday and Friday are the busiest days.

The Region: Altoona has been a rail center for almost a century and a half. The Pennsylvania Railroad founded the town in 1849, and it gained fame and prosperity when Horseshoe

Curve opened in 1854. The city still has a strong rail presence, but the economy has diversified over the years.

The surrounding region is mountainous and wooded. Most of the region's cities and towns lie in relatively narrow valleys in the mountains.

Schedule:
April through October—daily: 10 A.M. to 6 P.M.
November through March—daily (except Tuesdays): 10 A.M. to 5 P.M.
Funicular Schedule:
May through October—daily: 9:30 A.M. to 7:00 P.M.
November through April—daily (except Mondays): 10:00 A.M. to 4:30 P.M.

Special Events: Altoona Railfest, first weekend in October. This is an extravaganza featuring tours of the museum and former shops of the Pennsylvania Railroad, now used by Conrail, and rail excursions across Horseshoe Curve, plus a half-marathon sponsored by Altoona Hospital.

Entrance:	Museum	
Adults		$5.00
Seniors (62 and up)		$4.50
Children 3 to 12		$3.00
	Funicular Fares	
Adults		$3.50
Seniors (62 and up)		$3.00
Children 3 to 12		$1.50

Nearby Attractions: Gallitzin Tunnels; Seldom Seen Mine (see Mines chapter); Johnstown Incline (see Inclines chapter); Benzel's Pretzel Factory; Lakemont Park (amusement park)

Tourist Information: Cambria County Tourist Council, 111 Market St., Johnstown, PA 15901, telephone 800-237-8590; or, Allegheny Mountain Convention and Visitors Bureau, Logan Valley Mall, Route 220 and Goods Lane, Altoona, PA 16602, telephone 800-84-ALTOONA

Nearest Tourist Railroad: Amtrak across Horseshoe Curve; the Altoona Amtrak station is adjacent to the museum

Cresson—Allegheny Portage Railroad National Historic Site

Telephone: 814-886-6150

Location and Directions: The site is between Altoona and Johnstown. The entrance is off U.S. Route 22 at the Gallitzin exit.

The Museum's Story: Before the building of Horseshoe Curve, the Allegheny Portage Railroad carried passengers and freight across the highest ridges in the Allegheny Mountains. Elevations reach above 2,200 feet, rising over 1,000 feet from Altoona.

This amazing piece of engineering used a series of 10 inclined planes and 11 levels to carry boats up and down the mountain, connecting the Eastern and Western divisions of the Pennsylvania Mainline Canal. The portage railroad was 36 miles in length, and the journey was both exciting and scary.

Little of the actual railroad still exists. It ceased operation in 1857. However, a reconstruction of Incline 6 gives a good idea of how the system worked. A few parts of the original road do exist, though. The Staple Bend Tunnel, the oldest railroad tunnel in the United States, is on the site, as are the Lemon House, an 1830s tavern, and the Skew Arch Bridge, a bridge built in a twisted configuration to allow a wagon road to cross the railroad without adjusting its straight path up the mountain.

At Engine House 6, interactive exhibits provide answers to questions about the railroad. The visitor center has a 20-minute film presentation, models, artifacts, and exhibits. A picnic area and hiking trails are at the site.

The Region: Manufacturing and mining define this region. With its steep mountains, it's not friendly to agriculture. Johnstown was a major steel city, and Altoona was a railroad city.

Schedule:

Memorial Day to Labor Day—daily: 9 A.M. to 6 P.M.

Rest of the year—daily: 9 A.M. to 5 P.M.

Special Events:

Evening On the Summit (programs present Pennsylvania's

heritage through speakers and performers)—summer Saturdays

Heritage Hikes (park rangers lead hikers to hidden places on the site)—select Sundays, reservations required

Entrance: Free

Nearby Attractions: Altoona Railroaders Museum beside the Amtrak station in Altoona; Johnstown Incline (see Inclines chapter); Gallitzin Tunnels; Seldom Seen Mine (see Mines chapter)

Tourist Information: Cambria County Tourist Council, 111 Market St., Johnstown, PA 15901, telephone 800-237-8590; or Allegheny Mountain Convention and Visitors Bureau, Logan Valley Mall, Route 220 and Goods Lane, Altoona, PA 16602, telephone 800-84-ALTOONA

Nearest Tourist Railroad: Amtrak across Horseshoe Curve from the Altoona station—12 miles away

Scranton—Steamtown National Historic Site

Telephone: 717-340-5200

Location and Directions: Take Interstate 81 to Scranton. Take exit 53, the Central Scranton Expressway, and go west to the third traffic light. Turn left and go one and a half blocks. Pass the Steamtown Mall and turn left on Lackawanna Avenue. The Museum is #150.

The Museum's Story: Steamtown celebrates the steam locomotive and the life of towns that steam trains served. This federally-funded site is home to an extensive collection of steam locomotives and other rolling stock. In addition, a movie theater offers an excellent short film that documents the life of a railroad man in the first half of the 20th century.

The site is a restored yard area of the Delaware, Lackawanna & Western Railroad, a line that operated primarily in New York, New Jersey, and Pennsylvania.

Steamtown was originally a private collection housed in

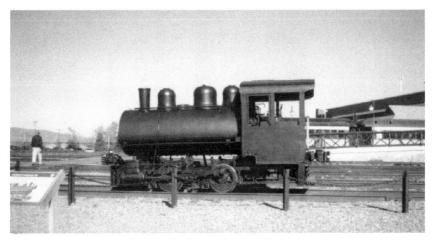

Steamtown National Historic Site.

Vermont. It came to Scranton when the federal government purchased it from the owner, and has provided an excellent railroad exhibit. Everything is first class, and the combination of National Park personnel and volunteers is an efficient and friendly one.

Steamtown's most impressive specimen is one of the Union Pacific Railroad's "Big Boy" locomotives, the biggest ever built. With its coal tender full, the Big Boy weighed in at 1,189,000 pounds. These locomotives did most of their work in the West, pulling heavy freight trains over Utah's Wasatch Mountains.

The Big Boy is just one of about 30 steam locomotives on the grounds. Some of the others are in the roundhouse, where visitors can see how trains change directions. The museum also houses a Technology Museum, a History Museum, and the Oil House, which now doubles as the gift shop.

The Region: See Steamtown National Historic Site entry in Northeast chapter

Schedule: Daily except Jan. 1, Thanksgiving, and Christmas: 9 A.M. to 5 P.M.

Special Events:

National Park Week—third week in April

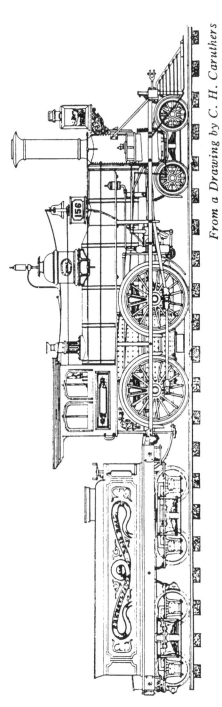

From a Drawing by C. H. Caruthers

American Type Passenger Locomotive, built by The Baldwin Locomotive Works, 1859

Courtesy Railroad Museum of Pennsylvania

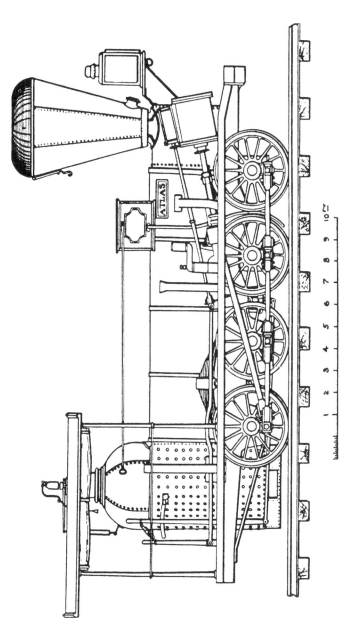

The "Atlas," Built by The Baldwin Locomotive Works, 1846

Courtesy Railroad Museum of Pennsylvania

Mother's Day Special
Veteran's Remembrance Special Event—10 days in mid-May
Father's Day Special
Toys for Tots Train—weekend after Thanksgiving
Entrance: Admission to the grounds is free.

Museum and Displays	
Adults	$6.00
Seniors	$5.00
Under 16	$5.00
Train rides	$8.00

Nearby Attractions: Pennsylvania Anthracite Heritage Museum; Scranton Iron Furnaces; Pocono Downs Race Track (harness racing); Pocono Raceway (auto racing); Lackawanna County Stadium (AAA baseball); Pocono Mountains

Tourist Information: Pennsylvania's Northeast Territory Visitors Bureau, 201 Hangar Rd., Suite 203, Avoca, PA 18641, telephone 800-22-WELCOME, web site http://www.travelfile.com

Nearest Tourist Railroad: Steamtown National Historic Site—same location; Stourbridge—30 miles away

Strasburg—Railroad Museum of Pennsylvania

Telephone: 717-687-7522

Location and Directions: Route 741 East

The Museum's Story: Pennsylvania is the focus of this museum. Almost every exhibit has a direct tie to the rails of the state. Pieces on display either operated in Pennsylvania or were built here. The museum houses approximately 100,000 archival items such as books and timetables, and 100,000 smaller artifacts. The core of the collection is the Pennsylvania Railroad's historical collection assembled for the 1938 World's Fair.

The Railroad Museum of Pennsylvania opened in 1974 and underwent an extensive expansion in 1995. It houses more than 80 engines and cars, some of which date back to the 1870s. Others come from the era of modern streamliners.

The Railroad Museum of Pennsylvania celebrates the mighty Pennsylvania Railroad.

Museum guides will take you through the facility and explain how steam engines worked and everything else that's pertinent to railroad history.

The Region: See Strasburg Railroad entry in Southeast chapter

Schedule: Daily (except New Year's Day, Veterans' Day, Thanksgiving, and Christmas, and Mondays during the winter months)—Monday through Saturday: 9 A.M. to 5 P.M.; Sunday: noon to 5 P.M.

Special Events: Pennsy Weekend—second weekend in June; plus different events announced each year

Entrance:

Adults	$6.00
Seniors (60 and up)	$5.00
Children 6 to 17	$4.00

Nearby Attractions: Choo-Choo Barn (model trains); National Toy Train Museum (see this chapter); Red Caboose Motel (see Resting chapter); Amish attractions

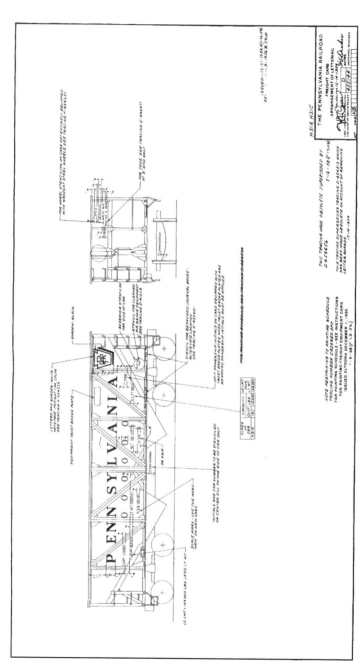

Courtesy Railroad Museum of Pennsylvania

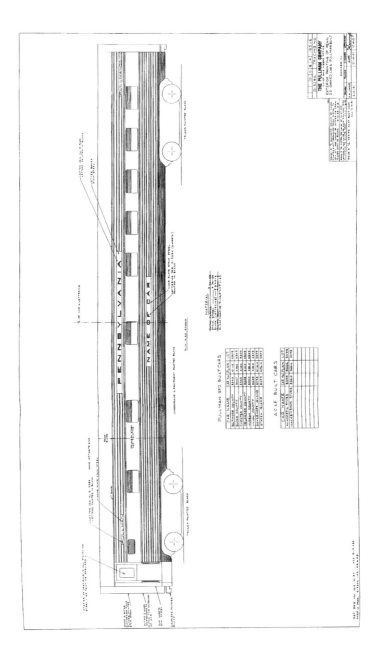

Courtesy Railroad Museum of Pennsylvania

Tourist Information: Pennsylvania Dutch Convention and Visitors Bureau, 501 Greenfield Rd., Lancaster, PA 17601, telephone 800-PA-DUTCH, web site http://www.800padutch.com
Nearest Tourist Railroad: Strasburg—across the street

Washington—Pennsylvania Trolley Museum

Telephone: 412-228-9256

Location and Directions: Washington is about 25 miles southwest of Pittsburgh on Interstate 79. From I-79, take exit 8 and follow the signs to the Trolley Museum at 1 Museum Rd. Be sure to follow the signs closely.

The Museum's Story: Trolleys carried millions of passengers before the automobile became the dominant mode of personal transportation. The Pennsylvania Trolley Museum recreates the trolley experience with displays, rides, pictorial exhibits, and films. Trolleys that operated in many parts of Pennsylvania and in many other parts of the country are on display and in operation. One car in the fleet is #832 from St. Charles Avenue in New Orleans, "The Streetcar Named Desire." Other readily recognizable cars come from Philadelphia and Pittsburgh. Volunteers rebuild trolleys, lay track, and serve as guides and trolley operators.

The Region: See Pennsylvania Trolley Museum entry in Trolleys chapter

Schedule: 11 A.M. to 5 P.M. on weekends, April through December, and 7 days a week, Memorial Day through Labor Day

Special Events:
Streetcar Named Desire Day—second Saturday in May
Trolley Fair—last weekend in June
Santa Trolley—three weekends following Thanksgiving
Trolleys and Toy Trains—weekend before Christmas and week between Christmas and New Year's Day

Entrance:

Adults	$5.00
Seniors (65 and up)	$4.00
Children 2 to 11	$3.00

The Pennsylvania Trolley Museum.

In a scene reminiscent of many American cities, streetcar tracks run through cobblestones.

Nearby Attractions: Meadows Race Track; Pennsylvania Arts and Crafts Country Festival (Memorial Day weekend); Washington County Fair (second full week of August); Washington County covered bridges (25)

Tourist Information: Washington County Tourism, 59 N. Main St., Washington, PA 15301, telephone 412-222-8130

Nearby Tourist Railroad: trolley rides on site; Laurel Highlands—50 miles away

Smaller Museums

Honesdale—Wayne County Historical Society Museum

Telephone: 717-253-3240

Location and Directions: 810 Main St., U.S. Route 6, 30 miles east of Scranton

The Museum's Story: The museum follows the history of Wayne County. An important part of that history centers on the railroad. A full-sized replica of the Stourbridge Lion is on display, and visitors can sit in a real Delaware & Hudson passenger car and watch a movie about the gravity railroad and the D & H Canal, which was part of the transportation system that carried coal from nearby mines to the major cities of the East Coast.

The Region: See Stourbridge Line entry in Northeast chapter

Schedule:

January, February—Saturday: 10 A.M. to 4 P.M.

March through June—Monday, Wednesday through Saturday: 10 A.M. to 4 P.M.

July through Labor Day—Monday, Wednesday through Saturday: 10 A.M. to 4 P.M.; Sunday: 12 noon to 5:00 P.M.

October through December—Monday, Wednesday through Friday: 1 to 4 P.M.; Saturday: 10 A.M. to 4 P.M.; first two Sundays of October: 12 noon to 5 P.M.

Special Events: None

Entrance: $3.00

Nearby Attractions: See Stourbridge Line entry in Northeast chapter

Tourist Information: See Stourbridge Line entry in Northeast chapter

Nearest Tourist Railroad: Stourbridge—on site

Leesport—Reading Technical and Historical Society

Telephone: 610-372-5513

Location and Directions: The museum is in Fleetwood, in northern Berks County. From Reading, go north on PA 61. At the light in Leesport, turn west. It's one block to the museum, at Wall and Canal streets.

The Museum's Story: The museum details the history of the Reading Railroad, which was once a powerful player in Pennsylvania. Many of its former lines now serve as tourist railroads. While the Reading was never as large or as powerful as the Pennsylvania Railroad, it was an important economic force in many Pennsylvania communities. The Reading even has a space in Monopoly.

Many pieces of rolling stock are on display, and occasionally the society runs excursions.

The Region: See East Penn entry in Southeast chapter

Schedule: Memorial Day weekend to Labor Day weekend—Saturday, Sunday: 12 noon to 5 P.M.

Special Events: None

Entrance: By donation

Nearby Attractions: See East Penn entry in Southeast chapter

Tourist Information: See East Penn entry in Southeast chapter

Nearest Tourist Railroad: East Penn—16 miles away

Manheim—Manheim Historical Society Railroad Station

Telephone: 717-664-3486

Location and Directions: This small museum, which also doubles as the Chamber of Commerce, is at 210 S. Charlotte St.

Manheim is in Lancaster County, in the southeastern part of the state. The museum lies just south of the Conrail tracks. To reach the museum from PA 72, Main Street, turn west on W. Stiegel Street. Go to the stop sign and go left on S. Charlotte Street.

The Museum's Story: This museum tells the stories of the community of Manheim and of trolleys and trains in Lancaster County. In addition to this, the museum offers the shortest trolley ride around, perhaps 100 yards. The museum has preserved a trolley car from the 1930s and stores it in a barn on the property. The trolley runs on a short stretch of track in front of the barn. While it would seem possible to tie into the lightly used Conrail tracks that are very close to the trolley's home, it isn't, because of the different gauges (track widths) used by those trains and this trolley. In addition to the trolley, several train cars are on display, as is an operating toy train layout.

The Region: See Strasburg entry in Southeast chapter
Schedule:
Museum—Saturday: 9 A.M. to 12 noon; Sunday: 1 to 4 P.M.
Trolley—by appointment
Special Events: None
Entrance: By donation
Nearby Attractions: See Strasburg entry in Southeast chapter
Tourist Information: See Strasburg entry in Southeast chapter
Nearest Tourist Railroad: Strasburg—17 miles away

Philadelphia—Transit Museum Store

Telephone: 215-580-7800
Location and Directions: The museum is at 1234 Market St. in Center City, about 3 blocks east of City Hall.

The Museum's Story: The Transit Museum has pictures and displays of streetcar service in Philadelphia. The museum also has an information desk and a store where visitors can buy books and souvenirs.

The Region: See Welcome Line entry in Trolleys chapter

Schedule: Monday to Friday: 9 A.M. to 5 P.M.; Saturdays: 10 A.M. to 5 P.M.; Sundays and holidays: closed
Special Events: None
Entrance: Free
Nearby Attractions: See Welcome Line entry in Trolleys chapter
Tourist Information: See Welcome Line entry in Trolleys chapter
Nearest Tourist Railroad: Welcome Line Trolley—in town

Robertsdale—East Broad Top Area Coal Miners Historical Society Miners Museum and Entertainment Center

Telephone: 814-635-3807
Location and Directions: Robertsdale is in Huntingdon County in southwestern Pennsylvania. It's a small town far from major highways. The simplest way to get there is to take the Pennsylvania Turnpike to exit 13, Fort Littleton. Go north on U.S. 522 to Orbisonia. Turn left on PA 994, which will take you to the East Broad Top Railroad. Continue west on 994 to Cooks. There, turn left on SR 3019, which will take you into Robertsdale.

The Museum's Story: The museum's story is one of coal mining and railroading. The story of the theater itself parallels the changes in mining towns. Robertsdale was the home of two movie houses during the 20th century. The Reality, where the museum now resides, was the second. Both struggled as coal mining declined. Now the Reality tells the story of an area that thrived on coal mining, iron making, and two major steam railroads—the standard gauge Huntingdon and Broad Top Mountain Railroad and the narrow gauge East Broad Top Railroad.

The Region: See East Broad Top entry in Southwest chapter
Schedule: Saturday: 10 A.M. to 5 P.M.; Sunday: 1 to 5 P.M.
Special Events: None
Entrance: Adults are $3.00 and children are $1.50.

Nearby Attractions: See East Broad Top entry in Southwest chapter

Tourist Information: See East Broad Top entry in Southwest chapter

Nearest Tourist Railroad: East Broad Top—16 miles away

Rockhill Furnace—Rockhill Trolley Museum

Telephone: 814-447-9576

Location and Directions: The Rockhill Trolley Museum is in Huntingdon County, adjacent to the East Broad Top Railroad. Take the Pennsylvania Turnpike to exit 13, Fort Littleton. Go north on U.S. 522 to Orbisonia. Go west on PA 994.

The Museum's Story: The museum tells the story of streetcars in the United States. Movies shown in the theater capture the feel of an era when trolleys were the primary means of transportation for millions of Americans. In those days tracks ran down the middle of many American streets. A wide variety of memorabilia, books, videos, and souvenirs is available in the store.

The museum's collection of trolleys resides in the shop. There you may see a vintage trolley from your hometown if you happen to hail from New Orleans, Philadelphia, Boston, or many other cities across the country. One of the most intriguing parts of all the trolleys is the advertising placards inside. Many of them are original and more than 50 years old.

The museum operates the Shade Gap Electric Trolley (see Trolleys chapter).

The Region: See East Broad Top entry in Southwest chapter

Schedule: Saturday: 10:30 A.M. to 5 P.M.; Sunday 10:30 A.M. to 4 P.M.

Special Events: None

Entrance: Adults are $3.00 and children (2 to 11) are $1.00.

Nearby Attractions: See East Broad Top entry in Southwest chapter

Tourist Information: See East Broad Top entry in Southwest chapter

Nearest Tourist Railroad: East Broad Top and Shade Gap Electric Railway—on site

Youngwood—Youngwood Railroad Museum

Telephone: 412-925-7355

Location and Directions: This museum is a stop on the Laurel Highlands Railroad. To reach it by motor vehicle, take U.S. 119 into Youngwood and turn east on Railroad Avenue.

The Museum's Story: This museum packs a large amount of history and memorabilia into a restored Pennsylvania Railroad Station. One of the highlights of this museum is a train whistle that children love but that can become annoying to adults after several hours of non-stop blowing. The museum also has an operating model train layout and adjacent picnic grounds.

The Region: See Laurel Highlands entry in Southwest chapter

Schedule: Tuesday through Saturday: 10 A.M. to 2 P.M. In addition, the museum is open whenever the Laurel Highlands Railroad is operating.

Special Events: None

Entrance: Free

Nearby Attractions: See Laurel Highlands entry in Southwest chapter

Tourist Information: See Laurel Highlands entry in Southwest chapter

Nearest Tourist Railroad: The Laurel Highlands, which begins 9 miles away, makes a stop at this museum.

Model Railroad Museums

Lehighton—Pocono Museum Unlimited

Telephone: 717-386-3117

Location and Directions: Lehighton is just south of Jim Thorpe on U.S. Route 209, along the Lehigh River. To reach the museum, go west on PA Route 443, Ashtown Drive, for ½ mile.

The Museum's Story: The museum houses a large collection of model trains. Sixteen trains run on more than 2,000 feet of track, recreating American scenes such as freight yards, small towns, big cities, and drive-in theaters.

The Region: See Rail Tours entry in Northeast chapter

Schedule:

May 1 to Labor Day—Wednesday through Monday: 12 noon to 5 P.M.

Rest of year—Saturday through Monday: 12 noon to 5 P.M.

Special Events: None

Entrance:

Adults	$4.00
Seniors (60 and up)	$3.00
Children 5 to 12	$2.00

Nearby Attractions: See Rail Tours entry in Northeast chapter

Tourist Information: See Rail Tours entry in Northeast chapter

Nearest Tourist Railroad: Rail Tours—six miles away

Shartlesville—Roadside America

Telephone: 610-488-6241

Location and Directions: Roadside America is on U.S. 22 in Berks County, fairly close to the East Penn and the Wanamaker, Kempton & Southern. Take exit 8, Shartlesville, from Interstate 78.

The Museum's Story: This display is a large exhibit of miniature towns showing the growth and history of rural America. Model trains are a major part of the display, which represents more than a half-century's work by the builder.

The Region: See Wanamaker, Kempton & Southern entry in Southeast chapter

Schedule:

July 1 to Labor Day—daily: 9:00 A.M. to 6:30 P.M.

Rest of the year—Monday through Friday: 10 A.M. to 5 P.M.; Saturday, Sunday: 10 A.M. to 6 P.M.

Special Events: None

Entrance: Adults are $3.75 and children (6 to 11) are $1.25.

Nearby Attractions: See Wanamaker, Kempton & Southern entry in Southeast chapter

Tourist Information: See Wanamaker, Kempton & Southern entry in Southeast chapter

Nearest Tourist Railroad: Wanamaker, Kempton & Southern—17 miles away

Strasburg—The National Toy Train Museum

Telephone: 717-687-8976

Location and Directions: The Toy Train Museum is on Paradise Lane, just east of the Strasburg Railroad. From Strasburg go east on PA 741 and make the first left past the Strasburg Railroad.

The Museum's Story: This museum is the national headquarters of the Train Collectors Association, a group whose mission is the preservation and history of toy trains. Five large layouts with push button controls are on display, as are many rare trains.

The Region: See Strasburg entry in Southeast chapter

Schedule:

May 1 through October 31—daily: 10 A.M. to 5 P.M.

April, November, early December—Saturday, Sunday: 10 A.M. to 5 P.M.

Also open the week after Christmas, the day after Thanksgiving, and Easter Friday and Monday, from 10 A.M. to 5 P.M.

Special Events: None

Entrance:

Adults	$3.00
Seniors (65 and up)	$2.75
Children 5 to 12	$1.50

Nearby Attractions: See Strasburg entry in Southeast chapter

Tourist Information: See Strasburg entry in Southeast chapter

Nearest Tourist Railroad: Strasburg—in town

Resting By the Rails

These places offer special treatment for rail fans.

Station Inn (Bed & Breakfast)

827 Front St., Cresson, PA 16630, 814-886-4757 (information) and 800-555-4757 (reservations)

Cresson is a small town in Cambria County, between Altoona and Johnstown. The region is home to many railroad attractions, including the busy Conrail line that runs 150 feet from the Station Inn's front porch.

Cresson is close to the highest point on the line, and from the inn you can see eastbound trains completing their climb to the Gallitzin tunnels and westbounds beginning their descent to Johnstown. Mail trains, merchandise trains, auto racks, coal drags, ore trains, double stacks, and Amtrak trains rumble by at all hours of the day. This may not be the ideal place if you're looking for complete quiet, but it's outstanding if you're looking for trains.

The Station Inn is not a luxury inn. It has no air conditioning, and no in-room phones or TV. The building is an 1866 railroad hotel, and the suites carry the names and colors of different railroads, such as the Pennsylvania and the Baltimore & Ohio. If you want to watch trains all night, ask for one of these two suites because they face the tracks.

The Station Inn is an excellent base for a train vacation, and it's open all year. These railroad attractions are nearby:

Allegheny Portage Railroad Museum (see Museums chapter)	2 miles
Gallitzin Tunnels	3 miles
Horseshoe Curve	9 miles
Altoona Railroader Museum (see Museums chapter) and Amtrak station	15 miles
Johnstown Incline (see Inclines chapter) and Flood Museum	20 miles
East Broad Top Railroad	60 miles

Red Caboose Motel

Paradise Lane, Strasburg, PA 17579, 717-687-500

The Red Caboose Motel lies right beside the tracks of the Strasburg Railroad, about ½ mile east of the station. All of the rooms at the Red Caboose are actual cabooses, and you can stay in a caboose from dozens of different railroads. Some can accommodate as many as 18 people, and they're all much more comfortable than they were when they rolled over the rails. On the grounds are a restaurant and gift shop.

Strasburg is in the heart of Amish country, and you'll see buggies go by more frequently than trains. In Strasburg you will find many railroad attractions besides the Strasburg Railroad:

• Choo-Choo Barn (model trains)
• Railroad Museum of Pennsylvania (see Museums chapter)
• National Toy Train Museum (see Museums chapter)
• Strasburg Train Shop

Casey's Caboose Stop Motel

221 South Monroe St., Titusville, PA 16354, 814-827-6597.

Located close to the Perry Street Station of the Oil Creek & Titusville Railroad, Casey's Caboose Stop offers 21 renovated cabooses that now serve as motel rooms. The rooms have modern features such as computer data ports. Adjacent to the motel is Molly's Mill, a renovated mill with an agricultural theme that now serves as a restaurant. Casey's Caboose Stop is within walking distance of the Perry Street Station.

Lackawanna Station Hotel

700 Lackawanna Ave., Scranton, PA 18503, 717-342-8300

Formerly the Delaware, Lackawanna & Western station, this majestic building is now a hotel. It received a multi-million dollar renovation in 1993, and Radisson now operates it. The building is French Renaissance style, with six imposing columns in front. Inside are a two and a half-story waiting room, Tiffany glass, and Siena marble.

The Lackawanna Station Hotel is just up the street from Steamtown (see Museums chapter), and the Stourbridge Line in Honesdale is 30 miles east on Route 6.

Train Vacations
Rail Travel Center Tours
2 Federal St.
Saint Albans, VT 05478
800-458-5394

Rail Travel Center Tours offers train vacations all over the world, including Pennsylvania. One recent tour included the Pittsburgh Inclines, the Knox & Kane Railroad, the Oil Creek & Titusville Railroad, Amtrak through Horseshoe Curve, the East Broad Top Railroad, and the Johnstown Incline.

Index